Traveler's Rede: Poetry from Hávamál

Max Ingram

OTHER BOOKS BY THIS AUTHOR

The Bone Forge, 2012
Horrors of death, madness and transformation lurk in the night.
From ancient gods left hanging on the gallows and cackling
demons that chase your steps, to the nightmare delusions of
insanity; this collection of horror themed poems will leave you
breathless and gasping in the dark.

The Endless Machine, 2015
Mysteries across space and time are waiting to be explored; from an
ancient alien migration, and romance with a starship, to space-suit
wearing angels falling from the stars. Prepare for a mind-altering
journey in The Endless Machine, the newest collection of science-
fiction poetry from Max Ingram.

COVER ART FOR TRAVELER'S REDE
by Karsten Schreurs
https://www.instagram.com/grobi_grafik

CONTENTS

ACKNOWLEDGMENTS

The following websites served as invaluable resources during the writing of this book.

The Database of Icelandic Morphology
https://bin.arnastofnun.is/DMII

Wiktionary, the free dictionary
https://en.wiktionary.org

Temple of Our Heathen Gods Resource Website
http://heathengods.com

TRAVELER'S REDE

INTRODUCTION

The book you're about to read is the result of a passion project that took nearly nine years to complete. And it all started with one (seemingly) simple question: What *exactly* does Hávamál say?

I'd long been a fan of the ancient, poetic text. It's a collection of home-spun wisdom put together in Iceland in the mid-to-late 1200's (but based on older, oral traditions - 'háva' = '<of> the High One / Odin,' 'mál' = 'words' or 'proverbs'). And though I had read multiple English translations, they frequently differed when it came to interpretation - sometimes drastically so. And oftentimes, they removed the poetic elements of the text - opting for plain English instead. This all left me with a feeling of dissatisfaction. And I would often find myself wondering what the text really said underneath it all.

So, it became a goal of mine (a bucket-list item, if you will), to learn Old Icelandic (sometimes called Old or Ancient Norse) sufficiently enough to read Hávamál in the original language and make up my own mind about its meaning. Well, that goal evolved over time to include much more, and became a desire to write the book you're about to read.

Herein, you will find:
- The first 80 stanzas of Hávamál, a section called Gestaþáttr by scholars because it focuses on advice pertaining to travelers ('gestr' = 'visitor/traveler,' 'þáttr' = 'section').
- A poetic rendering of these stanzas in a style similar to the ancient, alliterative form (though with some license taken).
- And a secondary, word-for-word English translation with explanatory notes and the original Icelandic shown.

In writing this book, I hoped to gain greater understanding of Hávamál, the ancient Norse culture that produced it, and the figure depicted as speaking its narrative (Odin, the Norse god of knowledge and wisdom). And I feel like I've achieved a measure of success with those goals (though sometimes I also feel I've only scratched the surface on all counts).

It's now my hope that in reading this book, you might gain the same. Or, at the very least, a collection of insightful and colorful advice from a bygone age, which may surprise you with its modern-day relevance.

Thank you for reading,
Max Ingram

ABOUT THE TRANSLATION

Hávamál, which translates as "Words (or Proverbs) of the High One," is a collection of 164 proverb-like stanzas which have been divided into five sections by scholars according to subject. Each stanza is written from the perspective of Odin, the Norse god of knowledge and wisdom, and aims to give advice on topics both mundane and esoteric.

Hávamál itself is one small part of a much larger text containing other collections of mythic and heroic poems from Norse culture. It was written in approx. 1260-1280 AD from earlier oral traditions, and variously called Konungsbók (The King's Book), Codex Regius (The Royal Manuscript), Eddukvæði (The Edda Poem), or simply The Elder or Poetic Edda. (The word 'edda' itself is a bit of a mystery, and may mean 'great-grandmother,' i.e. a person who relates old stories, or simply 'poem').

The original manuscript is written on vellum pages (fine parchment made from animal skin) and both compactly written and highly abbreviated for saving space (as vellum pages were costly to produce). This means that a page of the original text appears as a nearly unbroken block of writing, with no line-breaks and minimal spacing, only minimal punctuation employed (typically a single period mid-stanza and another at end of stanza), and with many words written in abbreviated forms similar to modern-day texting. The usage of definite and indefinite articles (such as 'a,' 'an,' and 'the') is also largely absent.

This, in part, explains the widely-varying presentations of different English translations of the text, as well as why some authors attribute different numbers to different stanzas. The original text assigns no numbers to the stanzas. The previous stanza ends with a period, while the next stanza begins with a capital letter; otherwise, there is no distinction between them.

The extensive use of abbreviations, in particular, presents a challenge for the translator, and means that many of the words must be guessed at, using a combination of context, grammar, and likelihood. So, in an effort to be as transparent about this process as possible, I have used the following symbols in my translation to indicate various insertions that were required.

[] = text inserted for clarity, but not present in the original manuscript. Conjectural.

<> = a meaning implied by the grammar on display, but not explicitly stated. Example: 'that <man>,' in which only the word 'that' is present, but the masculine grammar implies the subject is a man.

{} = a near, or conjectural synonym. Not an exact translation, but seems to fit the context more appropriately.

Note also that archaic or non-standard word spellings were sometimes employed in the manuscript, as well as special symbols (called sigla) in place of commonly used words (like the conjunction 'and'), and those have all been normalized in the original language portions to ease the reader's experience (as well as to better facilitate their own research, should they desire it).

Gestaþáttr Poems

STANZA 1

1.) At every archway,
2.) before one ambles forth,
3.) fain to look, they should be,
4.) to linger and gaze through door.
5.) Seldom 'twill be known,
6.) when seekers of one's death
7.) may dwell in darkness before.

ORIGINAL LANGUAGE

1.) Gáttir allar
([at] doorways - all)

2.) áðr gangi fram
(before - [one] goes - forth)

3.) u[m] skoðask skyli
(around - *look+oneself- should)

4.) u|m] skyggnast skyli.
(around - *spy+oneself - should)

5.) þvíat óvíst e[r] at vita
(because - uncertain - is - to - know)

6.) hvar óvin[ir]
(where - *enemies)

7.) sitja á fleti f[yrir].
(sit - in - rooms - before)

NOTES

1.3: The verb 'skoða' means 'to look, observe' or 'to examine' something, and when paired with the reflexive (i.e. self-referential) suffix and the prep. 'um,' the implied meaning seems to be 'look around oneself.'

1.4: The verb 'skygna' means 'to spy, peer' or 'to examine closely.' So while not an exact synonym with 'skoða' in line three above, it does have a very similar meaning. In fact, some translations merge lines three and four into a single line for the sake of brevity. I have chosen to preserve them in their original form instead.

1.6: The word 'óvinir' is most often rendered as 'enemies.' It consists of two parts, the negative prefix, and the plural form of the noun 'vinr' (friend), which comes out literally as 'un+friends' or 'not+friends.'

STANZA 2

1.) Lend ear to me, hosts!
2.) For here, a guest has fared,
3.) but whereabouts will they fit?
4.) Impatient is one
5.) who towards the hearth must
6.) muscle for a place to sit.

ORIGINAL LANGUAGE

1.) Gefendr heilir
(*{hosts} - blessed)

2.) gestr e[r] in[n] komi[nn]
(*visitor - is - within - come)

3.) hvar sk[al] sitja sjá.
(where - shall - sit - that <person>)

4.) mjök er bráðr
(greatly is *impatient)

5.) sá er á bröndu[m] sk[al]
(that <one> - who - towards - hearth - must)

6.) síns u[m] freista f[ra]ma.
(<for> their [own] - around - *vie - *placement)

NOTES

2.1: The noun 'gefendr' properly means 'givers' or '(those who) give,' but here I think the implication is 'hosts,' and that when paired with the adj. 'heilir' it's being used as a term of address for those who are about to give hospitality to a visitor (i.e. 'Blessed Hosts').

2.2: The noun 'gestr' can have a range of meanings. In the oldest sense, it simply meant 'a visitor,' (i.e. anyone who chances upon your doorstep, welcome or otherwise), 'a stranger' or 'traveler.' It was only later that it came to take on the meaning of '(a welcome or expected) visitor' and formed the basis for the modern English noun 'guest.'

2.4: The adj. 'bráðr' can mean 'hasty,' 'eager' or even 'hot-tempered,' but here I think it implies being 'impatient.'

2.6: This line is a bit tricky and open to interpretation. The verb 'freista' means 'to attempt' or 'try,' while the noun 'frama' can mean 'advancement' or 'benefit' (among other possibilities), but here I believe the line is attempting to say that a person will be left feeling greatly impatient if they must 'vie for their own placement' around the hearth. In other words, it's likely cold outside (hence the warm fire) and someone coming in from that cold should be shown directly to the warm hearth.

STANZA 3

1.) Of warmth, is needful,
2.) the one who comes within,
3.) when frozen they be, to knees.
4.) Of food and fresh garb,
5.) a guest will be needful,
6.) who's fared o'er mountains and trees.

ORIGINAL LANGUAGE

1.) Elds er þörf
(<of> fire - is - needful)

2.) þei[m]s in[n] er komi[nn]
(that <one>+who - within - is - come)

3.) ok á kné kalin[n].
(and - to - knees - frozen)

4.) matar ok váða
(<of> food - and - <of> clothing)

5.) er m[ann]i þörf
(is - person - needful)

6.) þeim e[r] hef[ir] u[m] fjall farit.
(that <one> - who - has - over - *mountain - fared)

NOTES

3.6: The noun 'fjall' is primarily used to mean 'a mountain,' but can also imply 'a fell,' which is 'an upland pasture, thicket' or 'highland plateau.'

STANZA 4

1.) Of wash, is needful,
2.) the one who comes to feast,
3.) fresh towel and fair bidding.
4.) A kind-hearted host,
5.) if have one, they can,
6.) and quiet, 'fore conversing.

ORIGINAL LANGUAGE

1.) Vat[n]s er þörf
(<of> *[washing] water - is - needful)

2.) þei[m] er t[il] v[er]ðar ke[m]r
(that <one> - who - to - meal - comes)

3.) þer[r]u ok þjóðlaðar.
(<of> towel - and - great+welcoming)

4.) góðs um æðis
(<of> [a host who is] good - of - disposition)

5.) ef s[ér] geta mætti
(if - <for> oneself - <to> get - is able)

6.) orðs ok endr þögu.
*(<of> conversing - and, yet - before - <of> quiet)

NOTES

4.1: The word used here is simply 'water,' but given the context of a person arriving after a long and arduous journey (stanza 3 mentions 'faring over mountain') I believe the implication is water to wash oneself with, particularly as a towel is mentioned as also being needful in line 3.

4.6: The meaning of this line is somewhat obscure and much-contested. Some take 'endr' and 'þögu' to be a compound word meaning either 'retribution' or 'silence in return.' Yet if both words are taken separately and translated at face value, they simply render as 'before - quiet.' If we also render the conjunction 'ok' in its rare, but acceptable interpretation as 'and, yet,' then we get the notion of the weary traveler needing 'conversation' from their host, and yet a period of quiet beforehand in which they can wash up and refresh themselves upon first arriving.

STANZA 5

1.) Of wits, is needful,
2.) the one who travels far,
3.) for much is well-known at home.
4.) One may garner stares,
5.) when understands little,
6.) yet among the wise does roam.

ORIGINAL LANGUAGE

1.) Vits er þörf
(<of> *wits - is - needful)

2.) þei[m] er víða ratar
(that <one> - who - widely - travels)

3.) dælt er heima hvat.
(familiar - is - at home - every[thing])

4.) at augabragði v[er]ð[r]
(*at+{stared} - becomes)

5.) sá e[r] ekki kan[n]
(that <one> - who - nothing - knows)

6.) ok m[eð] snotru[m] sitr.
(and, yet - among - [the] wise - sits)

15

NOTES

5.1: The noun 'vit' means 'wits,' 'intelligence,' or 'good sense,' 'wisdom.'

5.4: A translation of the compound 'auga-bragð' is '<of> [the] eye + sudden shift.' In some contexts, it's used to mean something happening very quickly or suddenly, i.e. in the blink of an eye, while in other contexts (particularly when paired with the prep. 'at') it's used to mean someone being 'stared' or 'glared at' (due to their doing something foolish or garnering mockery).

STANZA 6

1.) Of one's own insights,
2.) grandstanding ought not be,
3.) but rather reserved in way.
4.) Quiet and prudent,
5.) approach the doors of homes,
6.) where rare' the reserved are blamed.
7.) An ally more stout
8.) a soul may never have
9.) than heaps of good sense, once gained.

ORIGINAL LANGUAGE

1.) At hyg[g]jandi sin[n]i
(of - understanding - one's <own>)

2.) skylit ma[ðr] hræsin[n] v[er]a
(should+not - person - boastful - be)

3.) heldr gætin[n] at geði[.]
(rather - reserved - in - manner)

4.) þá e[r] horskr ok þögul[l]
(then - when - prudent - and - quiet)

5.) k[em]r heimisgarða til
([should] come - homestead+gates - to)

6.) sjaldan v[er]ðr víti vöru[m][.]
(seldom - befall - rebukes - [the] cautious)

7.) þ[ví]at óbrigð[an] vin
(because - [a more] unfickle - friend)

17

8.) fær m[aðr] aldregi
(gains - person - never)

9.) en man[n]vit mikit.
(than - *good sense - much)

NOTES

6.1-9: Though sentence structure would suggest that full stops (i.e. periods) should be present at the ends of lines 3 & 6, the manuscript displays no such punctuation. There is only a single full stop at the end of line 9.

6.9: The compound noun 'mann-vit' means 'the sense or reason of the (common) man, common sense; good sense.'

STANZA 7

1.) The wise visitor,
2.) who ventures to a feast,
3.) falls quiet, once closing door.
4.) With ears, they listen,
5.) and with eyes, they observe,
6.) so testing all truth before.

ORIGINAL LANGUAGE

1.) In[n] vari gestr
(the - *knowing - visitor)

2.) e[r] t[il] v[er]ðar ke[m]r
(who - to - meal - comes)

3.) þun[n]u hljóði þeg[ir].
(<for> acute - listening - is quiet)

4.) eyru[m] hlýð[ir]
(<with> ears - listens)

5.) en augu[m] skoðar
(yet - <with> eyes - observes)

6.) s[vá] nýsis[k] fróð[ra] hv[e]r[r] f[yrir].
(thus - investigates - *clever <one>+each - [what is] before)

19

NOTES

7.1: The adjective 'var' is somewhat open to interpretation, as it can mean 'wary' (i.e. 'cautious') or 'aware' (i.e. 'knowing'). And in this latter sense, it seems at times to be used in the sense of 'wise.' For this stanza, I am apt to lean toward the meaning of 'knowing' or 'wise,' as this concept seems reinforced in line 6 by the presence of the phrase 'fróðra hverr' (i.e. 'clever <one>+each').

7.6: The adjective 'fróðr' can have a range of meanings, which include 'educated (in a formal sense),' 'clever (in a positive sense), having quick intelligence,' 'skillful,' or even 'clever (in a negative sense), deeming oneself clever or skillful (while not truly being so); deeming oneself superior (while not truly being so).'

STANZA 8

1.) Fortunate, they are,
2.) who for themselves, achieve
3.) cheers and charitable writ.
4.) But harder is such
5.) which a person must have
6.) from the house where heart does sit.

ORIGINAL LANGUAGE

1.) Hin[n] e[r] sæll
(that <person> - is - fortunate)

2.) e[r] sér um getr
(who - oneself - for - gains)

3.) lof ok líknstafi.
(praise - and - <of> *{goodwill}+writings)

4.) ódælla er við þ[at]
(more difficult - is - regarding - that)

5.) er m[aðr] eiga sk[al]
(which - person - have - must)

6.) an[n]ars brjóstu[m] í.
(<of> another - [the] *breast - within)

NOTES

8.3: I found few references for 'líkn-stafi.' The Cleasby / Vigfusson Icelandic-English Dictionary makes no mention that I was able to find. While Zoëga's Concise Dictionary of Old Icelandic does mention it, but only as meaning 'good favour, comfort.' The noun 'líkn' means 'comfort' or 'charity,' while the noun 'stafi' is the plural of 'stafr,' and means 'staves,' but with the implication of 'written letters.' I think the intended meaning is 'writings + [of] goodwill,' or perhaps 'charitable / comforting writings (about one).' When 'líkn-stafi' is paired here with 'lof' ('praise'), I believe the intent is to describe both written and verbal accolades which people might heap upon one (perhaps even posthumously).

8.6: The noun 'brjóst' means 'breast' (i.e. the upper part of the chest, in both men and women). According to the Cleasby / Vigfusson Icelandic-English Dictionary, "With the ancients the breast was thought to be the abode of the mind, as well as of feeling...." So while we in modern times may attribute the faculty of thought to our brain, and our emotions in a metaphorical sense to our heart, it appears the ancient Norse had a different perception. To them, both thoughts and feelings originated in the breast, and so their word 'brjóst' can actually be interpreted differently depending on the context in which it is used, (e.g. as 'heart / feelings' or 'mind / reasoning').

STANZA 9

1.) Quite lucky are they
2.) who for themselves, secure
3.) good sense, in spite of praising.
4.) For guidance so poor
5.) oft gathers a person,
6.) from someone else's reas'ning.

ORIGINAL LANGUAGE

1.) Sá e[r] sæll
(that <person> - is - fortunate)

2.) er sjalfr u[m] á
(who - oneself - for - has)

3.) lof ok vit með[an] lif[ir].
([both] praise - and - *good sense - as long as - [they] live)

4.) þvíat ill ráð
(because - poor - advice)

5.) hef[r] m[aðr] oft þegit
(has - person - often - received)

6.) an[n]ars brjóstu[m] ór.
(<of> another - [the] *breast - from)

NOTES

9.3: The noun 'vit' means 'wits,' 'intelligence,' or 'good sense,' 'wisdom.'

9.6: The noun 'brjóst' means 'breast' (i.e. the upper part of the chest, in both men and women). According to the Cleasby / Vigfusson Icelandic-English Dictionary, "With the ancients the breast was thought to be the abode of the mind, as well as of feeling...." So while we in modern times may attribute the faculty of thought to our brain, and our emotions in a metaphorical sense to our heart, it appears the ancient Norse had a different perception. To them, both thoughts and feelings originated in the breast, and so their word 'brjóst' can actually be interpreted differently depending on the context in which it is used, (e.g. as 'heart / feelings' or 'mind / reasoning').

STANZA 10

1.) No finer burden
2.) bears a fellow by road
3.) than a rucksack full of sense.
4.) As finer than gold,
5.) it's gauged, in foreign place;
6.) for the downtrod', it's defense.

ORIGINAL LANGUAGE

1.) Byrði bet[ri]
(burden - better)

2.) berrat m[aðr] brautu at
(bears+not - person - road - upon)

3.) en sé man[n]vit mikit[.]
(than - is - *common sense - much)

4.) auði bet[ra]
(wealth - better [than])

5.) þyk[ki]r þ[at] í ókun[n]u[m] stað
(is deemed - it - in - un+familiar - place)

6.) slíkt e[r] válaðs vera.
(such - is - <for> [the] *distressed - shelter)

NOTES

10.3: The compound noun 'mann-vit' means 'the sense or reason of the (common) man, common sense; good sense.'

10.3: No full stop (i.e. period) is present at the end of line 3 in the manuscript, though sentence structure would suggest one should be.

10.6: The adjective 'válaðr,' which is derived from the verb 'vála' ('to weep; to wail'), properly means '(one who has) wept or wailed,' and by extension '(one who is) wretched, miserable, or distressed.' It can also simply mean '(one who is) needy or impoverished.'

STANZA 11

1.) No finer burden
2.) bears a fellow by road
3.) than a rucksack full of sense.
4.) No worse provision
5.) one pulls o'er wide grasses
6.) than ale that's overdrunk hence.

ORIGINAL LANGUAGE

1.) Byrði b[etri]
*(burden - better)

2.) b[errat maðr brautu at]
(bears+not - person - road - upon)

3.) [en sé mannvit mikit].
(than - is - *common sense - much)

4.) vegnest v[err]a
(road+provision - worse)

5.) veg[ra] h[ann] velli at
(carries+not - one - field - upon)

6.) en sé ofdrykkja öls.
(than - is - over+drinking - <of> ale)

NOTES

11.1-3: Lines 1 through 3 are significantly abbreviated in the manuscript, appearing simply as "Byrði b. b." This was sometimes done if the same section of text was being repeated in close proximity to a prior depiction, and these three lines also appear in stanza 10.

11.3: The compound noun 'mann-vit' means 'the sense or reason of the (common) man, common sense; good sense.'

STANZA 12

1.) Is not quite so fine
2.) as folks often declare,
3.) lager, for the likes of one.
4.) For less does one mind,
5.) when more does one consume,
6.) the soundness of what is done.

ORIGINAL LANGUAGE

1.) era svá gótt
(*is+not - so - good)

2.) sem gót[t] k[ve]ða
(as - good - is proclaimed)

3.) öl alda sona.
(ale - <for> *sons+<of> [this] generation)

4.) þvíat færa veit
(because - less *looks)

5.) er fleira drekkr
(when - more - drinks)

6.) síns t[il] geðs gumi[.]
(his <own> - to - *judgment - [a] *man)

NOTES

12.1: The manuscript does not depict this stanza as beginning with a capital letter, which is the standard way it would communicate the start of a new stanza. So, either the contents of stanzas 11 and 12 are meant to be read as a single, overlong stanza, or the scribe simply made a mistake.

12.3: The phrase 'alda sona,' if translated literally, reads as '[the] sons - <of> [a] time/age/period,' and might be interpreted as '[the] sons - <of> [this] generation,' or perhaps even more colloquially as 'people these days.' According to the Icelandic dictionaries of Cleasby / Vigfusson and Zoëga, it's a poetic turn-of-phrase meant to imply 'the sons of men,' (i.e. 'people' or 'humanity' in general).

12.6: "[a] man - looks - less - to - his <own> - judgment," i.e. he pays less attention to it, he does not hold it to the scrutiny he should.

12.6: In its oldest usage, the noun 'geð' can have a range of possible meanings, which include 'the mind,' 'the senses,' and 'the faculty of judgment.' In more modern usage, the word tends to be used for 'the emotional state of mind; mood, disposition, or even passion.'

12.6: The noun 'gumi' was used in Hávamál as a poetic stand-in for 'man,' but a literal translation is 'groom.' Related to the verb 'guma' and/or 'geyma' ('to keep, watch, mind'), the original sense is one of 'caretaker,' and was used in phrases like "brúð-gumi" = "groom (i.e. caretaker) - <of the> bride" and "hús-gumi" = "groom (i.e. caretaker) - <of the> house."

12.6: There is no full stop (i.e. period) visible in the manuscript at the end of line 6, though the next line does begin with a capital letter.

STANZA 13

1.) Dubbed the Unheeding,
2.) which hunts o'er draughts of ale;
3.) all good sense, it steals away.
4.) 'Neath that heron's wings,
5.) I was then wholly gripped,
6.) in Gunnlöð's 'bode, where I stayed.

ORIGINAL LANGUAGE

1.) Ómin[n]is hegri heit[ir]
(<of> *no+{mindfulness} - heron - is named)

2.) sá er yf[ir] öldru[m] þrum[ir]
(that <one> - who - over - ale feasts - *stands fast)

3.) h[ann] stelr geði guma.
(he - steals - [the good] *judgment - <of> man)

4.) þes[s] fugls fjöðru[m]
([beneath] that - bird's - feathers)

5.) ek fjötrað[r] vark
(I - caught - was)

6.) í garði Gun[n]laðar.
(in - dwelling - <of> *Gunnlöð)

NOTES

13.1: 'Óminni,' a compound of the noun 'minni' and a neg. prefix, might be taken two ways; as 'without + memory' or 'without + thought, consideration, care.' Given the context of this stanza, I favor the latter. Particularly if it's meant to depict Odin as regretting his misleading of Gunnlöð.

13.1: The heron (a long-legged, long-billed bird) hunts by standing motionless over a patch of water, and extends its wings over said water to produce shade. This shade makes it easier for the heron to spot its prey and serves to attract fish as they are drawn to shady areas. The shade-providing wings of the heron may represent the roof of the ale hall. And the fish drawn to that shade might mirror patrons looking for drink. The lunge of the heron's beak, snatching up its prey, represents the loss of a man's good judgment from drunkenness.

13.3: In its oldest usage, the noun 'geð' can have a range of possible meanings, which include 'the mind,' 'the senses,' and 'the faculty of judgment.' In more modern usage, the word tends to be used for 'the emotional state of mind; mood, disposition, or even passion.'

13.6: Gunnlöð was a giantess whom Odin encountered while seeking a taste of the poetic mead (i.e. the source of poetic inspiration). In exchange for three nights of passion, Gunnlöð allowed Odin three drinks of the mead. But Odin took superhuman-sized drinks, draining an entire crock each time, and consumed all the mead there was. Then he transformed into an eagle and flew away.

Gunnlöð's name is a compound, formed from the noun 'gunnr' ('war, battle') and the noun 'löð' ('bidding, invitation'). This might be interpreted as 'Inviter of Battle' or perhaps 'The Call of Battle.'

STANZA 14

1.) I thus became drunk,
2.) too drunk by far, I say,
3.) where the sage on mountain sits.
4.) A feast is thus best,
5.) when back from, may ferry,
6.) every fellow, their full wits.

ORIGINAL LANGUAGE

1.) Ölr ek varð
(drunk - I - became)

2.) varð ofrölvi
(became - too+drunk)

3.) at ins fróða fjalars[.]
(at - the - learned <one's> - <of> *the mountains)

4.) þ[ví] er ölðr baztr
(therefore - is - drinking party - best)

5.) at aftr of heimt[ir]
(which - back - from - brings home)

6.) hv[er]r sit[t] geð gumi[.]
(each - their <own> - *faculties - *man)

NOTES

14.3: 'Fjalar' is likely a title, rather than a name, and was applied to various figures in Norse mythology; a dwarf in a list of names (Völuspá 16), the giant Skrýmir (Hárbarðsljóð 26), a rooster who crows at Ragnarök (Völuspá 42), a giant in a list of names (Skáldskaparmál, pg. 156), and one of two dwarves who murder Kvasir (Skáldskaparmál, pg. 62 - Everyman edition).

This could be the old plural form of the noun 'fjöl' = 'thin boards' or 'snowshoes.' But I find this lacking. So, I propose two theories, both which assume an abbreviation of the noun 'fjall' ('mountain') has taken place.

The plur. genitive of 'fjall' is 'fjalla,' but if abbreviated and given a nominative 'r' (as a title might require), it could result in 'fjalar,' and would mean '<of> the mountains.' It might also be a compound of 'fjall' ('mountain') + 'ar' ('abundance'), and could result in 'wealth [of the] mountain.' Either makes sense when applied to dwarves and giants, as these figures are associated with jewels and metals, and depicted as living in or upon mountains. The giant Suttung (who may be the figure in stanza 14) has a daughter who lives inside a mountain and safeguards the mead of inspiration (see stanza 13).

14.6: In its oldest usage, the noun 'geð' can have a range of possible meanings, which include 'the mind,' 'the senses,' and 'the faculty of judgment.' In more modern usage, the word tends to be used for 'the emotional state of mind; mood, disposition, or even passion.'

14.6: The noun 'gumi' was used in Hávamál as a poetic stand-in for 'man,' but a literal translation is 'groom.' Related to the verb 'guma' and/or 'geyma' ('to keep, watch, mind'), the original sense is one of 'caretaker,' and was used in phrases like "brúð-gumi" = "groom (i.e. caretaker) - <of the> bride" and "hús-gumi" = "groom (i.e. caretaker) - <of the> house."

STANZA 15

1.) Quiet and cautious
2.) ought the noblest ones,
3.) and yet bold in battle, be.
4.) Joyful and giving
5.) should every good fellow,
6.) 'til passing from earth, proceed.

ORIGINAL LANGUAGE

1.) Þagalt ok hugalt
(quiet - and - careful)

2.) skyli þjóðans barn
(should - <of> *nobility - child)

3.) ok vígdjarft vera[.]
(*and yet - *battle+bold - be)

4.) glaðr ok reifr
(cheerful - and - *{generous})

5.) skyli gumna hv[er]r
(should - <of> *men - each [one])

6.) unz sin[n] bíð[r] bana.
(until that - time, - remain, - <of> death)

35

NOTES

15.2: The phrase 'þjóðans barn,' might be taken a few ways. If read literally, it means '<of> king/ruler - child.' However, the Cleasby / Vigfusson Icelandic-English Dictionary cites 'þjóðann' was sometimes used figuratively in poetry to mean "a good, a great man," perhaps alluding more to one's nobility of spirit rather than genealogy. And if that holds true here, then the phrase being used may be similar to 'alda sona' (which means 'sons of men,' but was a roundabout way of saying 'mankind'), making 'þjóðans barn' ('child of nobility') a roundabout way of saying 'a noble person.'

15.3: I believe the conjunction 'ok' (meaning 'and') is being used here in its less common, but still acceptable meaning of 'and yet,' as boldness is in direct contrast to cautiousness. I also believe this notion of being 'quiet and careful,' yet 'bold in battle' as well, is similar to the sentiment expressed by Theodore Roosevelt when he said, "Speak softly and carry a big stick."

15.4: The most common translation given for 'reifr' is 'glad, cheerful' (Cleasby & Zoëga), making it a synonym with 'glaðr' (which also means 'glad, cheerful'). But while 'glaðr' is related to the verb 'glaða' / 'gleðja' (meaning 'to make glad') and the noun 'gleði' (meaning 'gladness, merriment'), 'reifr' has a very different derivation and, I believe, a different meaning as well. The adjective 'reifr' is instead related to the verb 'reifa' (meaning 'to enrich, present with') and the noun 'reifir' (meaning 'a giver, helper'), thus perhaps making the adjective something closer to 'open (handed), generous.'

15.5: The noun 'gumi' was used in Hávamál as a poetic stand-in for 'man,' but a literal translation is 'groom.' Related to the verb 'guma' and/or 'geyma' ('to keep, watch, mind'), the original sense is one of 'caretaker,' and was used in phrases like "brúð-gumi" = "groom (i.e. caretaker) - <of the> bride" and "hús-gumi" = "groom (i.e. caretaker) - <of the> house."

STANZA 16

1.) The fainthearted ones
2.) will always live, they bode,
3.) if no battles, they will brave.
4.) But old age awards,
5.) to one, no lasting peace,
6.) although spears may choose to save.

ORIGINAL LANGUAGE

1.) Ósnjallr m[aðr]
(not+bold - person)

2.) hyg[g]s[k] munu ey lifa
(thinks+himself - will - forever - live)

3.) ef h[ann] við víg varas[k].
(if - he - against - *violence - *guards+himself)

4.) en elli gefr
(but - old age   grants)

5.) h[án]um engi f[ri]ð
(him - no - *peace)

6.) þót[t] h[án]um geirar gefi.
(though - him - spears - <may> grant)

NOTES

16.3: The noun 'víg,' which might be singular or plural as written here, means 'a fight, battle,' in the oldest sense. But it was also used as a law term for homicide (e.g. "any slaughter with a weapon, in open warfare and private feud," The Cleasby / Vigfusson Icelandic-English Dictionary). In modern Icelandic, the word has come to mean 'slaying, killing' in general. To be a sort of catch-all, I have rendered it here as simply "violence."

16.3: The reflexive usage of the verb 'vara' (normally meaning 'to warn') is used here to mean 'to guard+oneself (against),' with the implication of 'to keep+oneself (from), i.e. 'to shun.'

16.5: The noun 'friðr' means 'fellowship' or 'closeness' in its oldest sense, but also 'peace,' 'safety' and 'security' (as a result of shared fellowship). In some contexts, it can even denote 'sacredness' (of a season, or term), i.e. that which should not be violated, like the trust shared in fellowship.

STANZA 17

1.) Only a fool gawks
2.) when for gathering arrives,
3.) grumbles detached or stands fixed;
4.) and then all at once
5.) when a drink of ale shares,
6.) shown is their wanting of wits.

ORIGINAL LANGUAGE

1.) Kópir afglapi
(stares - [the] *beyond+diminished)

2.) er t[il] kyn[n]is ke[m]r
(when - to - social gathering - arrives)

3.) þylsk h[ann] um eð[a] þrum[ir].
(murmurs+himself - he - by - or - stands fixed)

4.) al[l]t er sen[n]
(all - happens - at once)

5.) ef h[ann] sylg um getr
(if - he - drink - of [ale] - gets)

6.) up[p]i er þá geð guma.
([shown] openly - is - then - *mind - <of> [that] *man)

NOTES

17.1: The compound 'af-glapi' means a person who is 'beyond + diminished,' with 'glapi' being the noun form of the verb 'glapna' which means 'to grow blunt or dim.' It seems to be a derogatory term meant to imply an 'utter fool' or 'complete idiot.'

17.6: In its oldest usage, the noun 'geð' can have a range of possible meanings, which include 'the mind,' 'the senses,' and 'the faculty of judgment.' In more modern usage, the word tends to be used for 'the emotional state of mind; mood, disposition, or even passion.'

17.6: The noun 'gumi' was used in Hávamál as a poetic stand-in for 'man,' but a literal translation is 'groom.' Related to the verb 'guma' and/or 'geyma' ('to keep, watch, mind'), the original sense is one of 'caretaker,' and was used in phrases like "brúð-gumi" = "groom (i.e. caretaker) - <of the> bride" and "hús-gumi" = "groom (i.e. caretaker) - <of the> house."

STANZA 18

1.) That fellow will know,
2.) who's wandered far and near,
3.) and fair hardships, underwent,
4.) what steady impulse
5.) each person is steered by,
6.) and whosoever has sense.

ORIGINAL LANGUAGE

1.) Sá ein[n] veit
(that <person> - alone - is aware)

2.) e[r] víða ratar
(who - widely - travels)

3.) ok hef[r] fjölð um farit.
(and - has - much - through - *endured)

4.) hv[er]ju geði
([by] what - *{motive})

5.) stýr[ir] gu[m]na hv[er]r
(<is> governed - <of> *men - each [one])

6.) sá er vitandi er vits.
([and] that <one> - who - knowing - is - <of> *sense)

41

NOTES

18.3: The sentiment in line 3 is sometimes translated literally, with the past participle 'farit' being employed as 'fared, journeyed' (e.g. through many places), but that would make it a simple repetition of the sentiment in line 2 (i.e. "who widely travels"), which I find unsatisfying. The verb 'fara' can also be used to mean 'suffer' or 'experience,' and if used in that manner instead, we get 'suffered, endured' (e.g. through many things), and a more satisfying accompaniment to line 2.

18.4: In its oldest usage, the noun 'geð' can have a range of possible meanings, which include 'the mind,' 'the senses,' and 'the faculty of judgment.' In more modern usage, the word tends to be used for 'the emotional state of mind; mood, disposition, or even passion.'

18.5: The noun 'gumi' was used in Hávamál as a poetic stand-in for 'man,' but a literal translation is 'groom.' Related to the verb 'guma' and/or 'geyma' ('to keep, watch, mind'), the original sense is one of 'caretaker,' and was used in phrases like "brúð-gumi" = "groom (i.e. caretaker) - <of the> bride" and "hús-gumi" = "groom (i.e. caretaker) - <of the> house."

18.6: The noun 'vit' means 'wits,' 'intelligence,' or 'good sense,' 'wisdom.'

STANZA 19

1.) In your mug, drown not;
2.) have drink, but in measure.
3.) Speak needful or be silent.
4.) And for such failing,
5.) no fellow should decry,
6.) if early to sleep you went.

ORIGINAL LANGUAGE

1.) Haldit m[aðr] á keri
(cling+not - person - to - cup)

2.) drekki þó at hófi mjöð.
(drink - although - in - moderation - mead)

3.) mæli þarft eð[a] þegi.
(speak - *necessary [words] - or - be silent)

4.) ókyn[n]is þ[es]s
(*unsociableness - <for> such)

5.) vár þik engi m[aðr]
(*[should] blame - you - no - person)

6.) at þú gang[ir] snem[m]a at sofa.
(that - you - go - early - to - sleep)

NOTES

19.3: The adjective 'þarft' ('necessary') has no noun to pair itself with. So I surmise the line is meant to imply 'necessary [words].'

19.4: The compound 'ó-kynni' is 'kynni' with a neg. prefix. The noun 'kynni' means 'closeness, familiarity,' but can also mean 'sociability, friendliness,' or perhaps even 'hospitality.' In some contexts, it can also mean 'a social visit (to a close friend or kinsman).'

19.5: Some render this line as a definite statement, e.g. "No person will blame you...." But as many can attest, some absolutely will blame you for leaving a party early, especially if you declare your intentions for sleep. In fact, doing so is practically an invitation for criticism in some circles. So for Hávamál to state unequivocally that such a thing will not occur, would be odd. I think, rather, this line implies "No person [should] blame you...."

STANZA 20

1.) The gluttonous one,
2.) unless their motive, gleans,
3.) gorges themselves t'ward sorrow.
4.) Oft contempt, provokes,
5.) when 'mong the prudent comes,
6.) belly of careless fellow.

ORIGINAL LANGAUGE

1.) Gráðugr halr
(gluttonous - *man)

2.) ne[m]a geðs viti
(unless - <of> *{motive} - has understanding)

3.) etr sér aldrtrega[.]
(eats - oneself - [to] lifetime + <of> sorrow)

4.) oft fær hlægis
(often - receives - ridicule)

5.) er m[eð] horsku[m] ke[m]r
(when - among - <the> prudent - arrives)

6.) man[n]i heimsku[m] magi.
*([the] man - heedless, - [his] stomach)

NOTES

20.1: The noun 'halr' was used in Hávamál as a poetic stand-in for 'man,' but a literal translation is 'hero' or 'person of great bravery,' and the word may be related to, or a synonym with 'höldr,' which was a term used for a social class of free landowners.

20.2: In its oldest usage, the noun 'geð' can have a range of possible meanings, which include 'the mind,' 'the senses,' and 'the faculty of judgment.' In more modern usage, the word tends to be used for 'the emotional state of mind; mood, disposition, or even passion.'

20.3: No full stop (i.e. period) is present in the original manuscript at the end of line 3, though grammar implies one should be present.

20.6: Sentence structure is a bit tortured here, with 'stomach' in the nominative (as the subject of the clause) and 'heedless man' in the dative (as an indirect object), but I believe it goes: '[His] stomach often receives ridicule, when [the] heedless man arrives among <the> prudent."

STANZA 21

1.) Even herds perceive
2.) the time to leave t'ward home
3.) and wander will from pasture.
4.) But a careless soul
5.) seldom will truly know,
6.) of their stomach, the measure.

ORIGINAL LANGUAGE

1.) Hjarðir þ[at] vitu
(herds - that - perceive)

2.) nær þær hei[m] skulu
(reach - they - *home [before sunset] - must)

3.) ok ga[n]ga þá af grasi.
(and - walk - then - from - grass)

4.) en ósvið[r] m[aðr]
(but - heedless - person)

5.) kan[n] ævagi
(understands - never)

6.) síns u[m] máls maga.
(their <own> - regarding - *{limits} - <of> stomach)

NOTES

21.2: Most cattle are left in pasture around the clock, and the animals simply congregate in a more protected area for nighttime sleeping. But dairy cattle are different, and need to be milked twice a day; once at sunrise and again around sunset. Because of this, dairy cattle are known to leave pasture, on their own, about an hour before sunset, and head back to homestead for milking.

Cattle reportedly eat five meals per day; a large one in the morning, another in the evening, and three smaller meals interspersed through the afternoon. To many observers, these animals may appear to be eating all day long. Yet, despite this seeming preoccupation with grazing, they still manage to know - by instinct - when to stop and start heading home.

The stanza doesn't specify what type of herd animal is being referenced, but I think it's safe to assume they were used for milking. Sheep were more commonly kept in Iceland (even for milk production), while on the mainland it would have been cattle.

21.6: The noun 'mál' means 'measurement' or 'dimensions,' but I think it's being used here to denote the physical limits of one's stomach.

STANZA 22

1.) That soul, unhappy,
2.) with a hateful swagger,
3.) will mock each one by laughing.
4.) They fail to know this,
5.) which they need to fathom,
6.) their flaws surely aren't lacking.

ORIGINAL LANGUAGE

1.) Vesall m[aðr]
(*un+happy - person)

2.) ok illa skapi
(and - [with] *{foul} - demeanor)

3.) hlær at hvívetna.
(laughs - at - every+being/thing)

4.) hit[t]ki h[ann] veit
(that+not - he - knows)

5.) er h[ann] vita þyrfti
(which - he - <to> know - needed)

6.) at h[ann] er[a] vam[m]a vanr.
(that - he - *is+not - <for> faults - lacking)

NOTES

22.1: The adjective 've-sall,' formed from 'saell' ('blessed; happy') and a negating prefix, means 'wretched, miserable,' 'deprived of (something),' or simply 'unhappy.'

22.2: The adjective 'illr' can mean 'ill, bad (in a bodily and moral sense),' 'poor (of quality),' 'difficult' or even 'stingy.'

22.6: There is likely an error in the manuscript here. Unaltered, it says "[the unhappy man] ...is lacking faults," when clearly it should say "...is *not* lacking faults." This involves adding a negative suffix to the verb 'er' in line 6, making it 'era.'

STANZA 23

1.) The foolhardy one
2.) is awake the whole eve,
3.) and upon each thing, they dwell.
4.) That one is then drained
5.) when daybreak does arrive,
6.) yet all is still woe as well.

ORIGINAL LANGUAGE

1.) Ósvið[r] m[aðr]
(un+wise - person)

2.) vakir u[m] allar nætr
(is awake - through - whole - night)

3.) ok hyg[g]r at hvívetna.
(and - thinks - upon - every+being/thing)

4.) þá er móðr
(then - is - exhausted)

5.) er at mor[g]ni ke[m]r
(when - to - morning - comes)

6.) al[l]t er víl se[m] var.
([yet] all - is - *misery - as - was)

NOTES

23.6: Odd usage here of a noun ('víl' = 'misery') rather than an adjective which would seem more appropriate. This may simply be poetic license.

STANZA 24

1.) A foolhardy soul
2.) assumes all folk, with them,
3.) who laugh along, are allies.
4.) They do not fathom,
5.) yet foul is spoke of them,
6.) when sit 'mong the sage, they try.

ORIGINAL LANGUAGE

1.) Ósnotr m[aðr]
(un+wise - person)

2.) hyg[g]r sér alla v[er]a
(believes - <with> himself - all - <to> be)

3.) viðhlæjendr vini.
(*who+laugh+along - friends)

4.) hit[t]ki h[ann] fið[r]
(that+not - he - perceives)

5.) þót[t] þ[ei]r um h[ann] fár lesi
(although - they - about - him - mischief - talk)

6.) ef h[ann] m[eð] snotru[m] sitr.
(if - he - among - <the> learned - sits)

NOTES

24.3: The compound adjective 'við-hlæj-endr' is comprised of the following elements; the prep. 'við' meaning 'along with,' the verb 'hlæja' meaning 'to laugh,' and the suffix '-endr' meaning 'one who does.' Once assembled, it appears to mean 'one who+laughs+along with.'

STANZA 25

1.) A foolhardy soul
2.) assumes all folk, with them,
3.) who laugh along, are allies.
4.) But soon discover,
5.) when venture to council,
6.) that few supporters they find.

ORIGINAL LANGUAGE

1.) Ósnotr m[aðr]
*(un+wise - person)

2.) h[yggr] s[ér] a[lla] v[era]
(believes - <with> himself - all - <to> be)

3.) v[iðhlæjendr] v[ini].
(*who+laugh+along - friends)

4.) þá þ[at] fin[n]r
(then - that - finds)

5.) er at þi[n]gi ke[m]r
(when - to - *assembly - comes)

6.) at h[ann] á formælendr fá[a].
(that - he - has - *who+speak+for [him] - few)

NOTES

25.1-3: In the manuscript, the first three lines are heavily abbreviated as "Osnotr m. h. s. a. v. v. vini." This is due to their being a repetition of the same lines used in stanza 24.

25.3: The compound adjective 'við-hlæj-endr' is comprised of the following elements; the prep. 'við' meaning 'along with,' the verb 'hlæja' meaning 'to laugh,' and the suffix '-endr' meaning 'one who does.' Once assembled, it appears to mean 'one who+laughs+along with.'

25.5: A 'þing' (pronounced as 'thing') was a general assembly in early Germanic societies. A variety of activities could take place at a 'þing' ranging from simple commerce to the settlement of disputes between clans and even the election of new public officials.

25.6: The compound 'for-mæl-endr' is comprised of three parts; the prefix 'for-' which is derived from the preposition 'fyrir' and means 'for' or 'before,' the verb 'mæla' meaning 'to speak,' and the suffix '-endr' which here serves to transform the verb 'mæla' into a noun meaning 'speakers' or 'those who speak.' Taken all together, it should come out as something like 'those who+speak+for,' (i.e. vocal supporters).

STANZA 26

1.) A foolhardy soul
2.) assumes they all fathom,
3.) if refuge in corner, keep.
4.) But discern, they not,
5.) what they need to answer,
6.) if answers do others seek.

ORIGINAL LANGUAGE

1.) Ósnotr m[aðr]
(un+wise - person)

2.) þykkis[k] al[l]t vita
(deems+himself - all - <to> know)

3.) ef h[ann] á s[ér] í vá veru.
(if - he - has - <for> himself - in - corner - shelter)

4.) hit[t]ki h[ann] veit
(that+not - he - knows)

5.) h[v]at h[ann] sk[al] við k[ve]ða
(what - he - must - with - *answer)

6.) ef h[an]s freista firar.
(if - <of> him - test - *people)

NOTES

26.5: The verb 'kveða' normally means 'to say,' though I think it might more properly be interpreted as 'to proclaim' with variations based on context (e.g. to proclaim (words), to say; to proclaim (a song), to sing; to proclaim (a verse), to compose; to proclaim (loudly), to scream or cry out). And when paired with the preposition 'við' (meaning 'with'), I believe it's meant to imply 'to proclaim (a response), to answer with, or reply.'

26.6: The plural noun 'firar' was used in Hávamál as a poetic stand-in for 'men, people,' but the literal meaning of this word is uncertain. The Linguistics Research Center of The University of Texas at Austin theorizes it may derive from the Proto-Germ. noun 'perku-s' meaning 'oak.' And this could make sense given the Norse conception of people as being crafted by the gods from wood. But I also theorize 'firar' may be a loan word derived from the Scottish Gaelic noun 'fear' (plural 'fir'), which itself is theorized as deriving from the Proto-Indo-Eur. noun 'wiHrós' ('man; husband; warrior, hero') and the root verb 'weyh-' ('to hunt'). And as such, 'firar' might mean 'hunters.'

STANZA 27

1.) For the unlearned soul,
2.) who steps amid large group,
3.) 'tis greatest if lips are sealed.
4.) No one discovers
5.) they understand little,
6.) lest speaking too much reveals.

*[or] (a possible tradition variant)

7.) As this one sees not,
8.) whose knowledge is wanting,
9.) what speaking too much reveals.

ORIGINAL LANGUAGE

1.) Ósnotr [maðr]
(un+learned - *[person])

2.) er m[eð] aldir ke[m]r
(who - among - many people - arrives)

3.) þ[at] er bazt at h[ann] þegi.
(it - is - best - that - he - is quiet)

4.) e[n]gi þ[at] veit
(no one - it - perceives)

5.) at h[ann] ekki kan[n]
(that - he - nothing - understands)

6.) ne[m]a h[ann] mæli t[il] mar[g]t.
(unless - he - *speaks/reveals - too - much)

59

7.) veita m[aðr]
*(perceives+not - person)

8.) hin[n] er vet[t]ki veit
(that <one> - who - nothing - understands)

9.) þót[t] h[ann] mæli t[il] mar[g]t.
(despite+that - he - *speaks/reveals - too - much)

NOTES

27.1: In the manuscript, the word 'maðr' ('person') is not present in line one. However, it seems likely the word was intended to be present, as the structure of the poem would be left uneven without it. Such an error would be simple to make as the scribal abbreviation used to represent the word 'maðr' is only a single character in length.

27.6 & 9: The verb 'mæla' can mean 'to speak' or 'to express, reveal (something).'

27.7-9: According to David A. H. Evans' commentary on the text, the German medievalist Helmut de Boor "...plausibly suggests that lines 4-6 and 7-9 are interchangeable tradition-variants." I take this to mean that more than one version of this stanza's latter half may have existed in oral traditions, and that when scholars recorded it, they may have chosen to do so by listing both versions of that ending, one after the other. This makes sense, as the majority of stanzas in this poem are six lines in length (w/ minor exceptions) and lines 4-6 and 7-9 are structurally similar. (Note that some translators have chosen to omit these latter three lines entirely from their interpretation of the text. While others include them, but perceive them as a continuation or commentary of the preceding lines.)

STANZA 28

1.) Think themselves clever,
2.) who discover gossip
3.) and voice the very same.
4.) Yet seldom conceal,
5.) can descendants of man,
6.) much that passes between them.

ORIGINAL LANGUAGE

1.) Fróðr sá þykkis[k]
(*clever - that <person> - deems+themself)

2.) e[r] fregna kan[n]
(who - <to> *hear [gossip] - is able)

3.) ok segja it sama.
(and - repeat - the - same)

4.) eyvitu leyna
(not at all - conceal)

5.) megu ýta syn[ir]
(may - <of> *men - sons)

6.) þv[í] er gengr u[m] guma.
(that - which - passes - between - *men)

NOTES

28.1: The adjective 'fróðr' can have a range of meanings, which include 'educated (in a formal sense),' 'clever (in a positive sense), having quick intelligence,' 'skillful,' or even 'clever (in a negative sense), deeming oneself clever or skillful (while not truly being so); deeming oneself superior (while not truly being so).'

28.2: The manuscript does not specify what is being heard and repeated by the listener, presumably because the composer assumed the audience could discern that from context. But given that it's something that commonly "passes between people," and is not deemed special, I believe it to be gossip. Note that similar phrasing of "fregna ok segja" ("hear and repeat [the same]") is also used in stanza 62, where I believe the subject to be gossip as well.

28.5: The phrase 'ýtar synir,' if translated literally, reads as '[the] sons - <of> voyagers' (from the verb 'ýta' meaning 'to launch, start on a voyage'). According to the Icelandic dictionaries of Cleasby / Vigfusson and Zoëga, it's a poetic turn-of-phrase meant to imply 'the sons of men,' (i.e. 'people' or 'humanity' in general).

28.6: The noun 'gumi' was used in Hávamál as a poetic stand-in for 'man,' but a literal translation is 'groom.' Related to the verb 'guma' and/or 'geyma' ('to keep, watch, mind'), the original sense is one of 'caretaker,' and was used in phrases like "brúð-gumi" = "groom (i.e. caretaker) - <of the> bride" and "hús-gumi" = "groom (i.e. caretaker) - <of the> house."

STANZA 29

1.) So often will crow,
2.) one who's seldom quiet,
3.) quarrelsome or foolish speech.
4.) A swift-wagging tongue,
5.) unless soundly restrained,
6.) often pulls trouble in reach.

ORIGINAL LANGUAGE

1.) Ærna mælir
(plenty of - speaks)

2.) sá er æva þeg[ir]
(that <one> - who - never - is quiet)

3.) staðlausu stafi.
(*{foolish} - *words)

4.) hraðmælt tu[n]ga
(swift+spoken - tongue)

5.) ne[m]a haldendr eigi
(unless - *bindings - has)

6.) oft s[ér] ógót[t] um gelr.
(often - itself - *mis+fortune - upon - *calls)

NOTES

29.3: A literal translation of the noun 'stafr' is 'stick' (a length of wood). But in the plural it sometimes implies 'written symbols' or 'wisdom,' meanings which originate in the ancient practice of carving runes into the surfaces of small sticks of wood used for divination. In instances where the 'stafir' are clearly being spoken, it can also mean 'words.'

29.3: The adjective 'staðlauss' means 'unsteady, groundless,' so when paired with 'stafr' ('written symbols,' 'wisdom,' or 'words'), it can mean 'unsound - wisdom,' 'senseless - words' or perhaps 'foolish - words.' And given the context of this stanza, I lean toward the latter.

29.5: I believe 'hald-endr' to be the verb 'halda' ('to hold') paired with the suffix '-endr' which converts it to a noun, resulting in 'holders' or 'bindings.'

29.6: The word 'ó-gótt' is the adjective 'góðr' ('good,' 'favorable') paired with a negative prefix. Translated literally, it comes out as 'un-favorable' or 'not-good.' But, when rendered in its neuter form, the adjective is often interpreted as a noun-like usage, coming out as 'evil' or 'misfortune.'

29.6: The verb 'gala' means (of a rooster) 'to crow,' but metaphorically 'to chant, sing,' 'to cry or call out.'

STANZA 30

1.) With a mocking glare,
2.) gaze upon no other,
3.) though pray for charity, they.
4.) Some think themselves high,
5.) if happen to be safe,
6.) and secure 'neath roof, they stay.

ORIGINAL LANGUAGE

1.) At augabragði
(*at+{glare})

2.) skala m[aðr] an[n]an hafa
(should+not - person - another - maintain)

3.) þót[t] t[il] kyn[n]is ko[m]i.
(despite+that - for - *{hospitality} - <may> come)

4.) margr þá f[ró]ðr þykkis[k]
(many [a person] - then - *{superior} - deems+himself)

5.) ef h[ann] fregin[n] er at
(if - he - *tested [by hardship] - is - not)

6.) ok nái h[ann] þur[r]fjallr þruma.
(and - is - able - he - *dry+skinned - <to> sit firm)

NOTES

30.1: A translation of the compound 'auga-bragð' is '<of> [the] eye + sudden shift.' In some contexts, it's used to mean something happening very quickly or suddenly, i.e. in the blink of an eye, while in other contexts (particularly when paired with the prep. 'at') it's used to mean someone being 'stared' or 'glared at' (due to their doing something foolish or garnering mockery).

30.3: The meaning intended for the noun 'kynni' in this passage is somewhat unclear. And it's been interpreted various ways by different authors. I believe at its core, the noun 'kynni' means 'closeness, familiarity,' but can also mean 'sociability, friendliness,' or perhaps even 'hospitality.' In some contexts, it can also mean 'a social visit (to a close friend or kinsman).'

30.4: The adjective 'fróðr' can have a range of meanings, which include 'educated (in a formal sense),' 'clever (in a positive sense), having quick intelligence,' 'skillful,' or even 'clever (in a negative sense), deeming oneself clever or skillful (while not truly being so); deeming oneself superior (while not truly being so).'

30.5: The adj. 'freginn' is a past participle of the verb 'fregna,' which most commonly means 'to hear, to learn.' But in older poetic usages, it sometimes meant 'to ask, to question, to test (a person's knowledge).' Here, the usage may be metaphorical, implying 'tested [by hardship].'

30.6: The adj. 'þurr-fjallr' comprises the adj. 'þurr' ('dry') and the noun 'fjall' ('the hide of an animal') and may indicate one's clothing (i.e. animal hides) or perhaps own personal skin is kept dry due to being sheltered from the elements.

STANZA 31

1.) Some think themselves high,
2.) who endeavor to smirk,
3.) so guest at guest is mocking.
4.) But seldom will know,
5.) the one who grins at sup,
6.) if wrathful souls they're scoffing.

ORIGINAL LANGUAGE

1.) Fróðr þykkis[k]
(*{superior} - deems+themself)

2.) sá e[r] flotta tekr
(that <one> - who - <to> *sneer - undertakes)

3.) gestr at gest hæðin[n].
([so that] guest - at - guest - [is] mocking)

4.) veita görla
([but] perceives+not - clearly)

5.) sá er u[m] verði glissir
(that <person> - who - over - meal - *grins/sneers)

6.) þót[t] h[ann] m[eð] grömu[m] glami.
(though - he - amid - <the> *wrathful - <may> *talk rowdily)

NOTES

31.1: The adjective 'fróðr' can have a range of meanings, which include 'educated (in a formal sense),' 'clever (in a positive sense), having quick intelligence,' 'skillful,' or even 'clever (in a negative sense), deeming oneself clever or skillful (while not truly being so); deeming oneself superior (while not truly being so).'

31.2: In the manuscript, the word written is simply 'flotta,' with no particular accenting. It's typically interpreted as the noun 'flótta' ('flight, fleeing'). But as mentioned by David A. H. Evans, the phrase 'taka flótta' ('take to flight') "does not seem to appear elsewhere" in the literature. And Guðmundur Finnbogason proposes an alternative in the form of an unrecorded Icelandic cognate 'flátta,' which equates to the Norwegian verb 'flåtta' ('to sneer at') and would be pronounced as 'flow-ta,' thus making a phonetic spelling of 'flotta' reasonable. Note that lines 5 & 6 may also contain evidence of a Norwegian dialectal influence.

31.5-6: According to David A. H. Evans, the verbs 'glissa' and 'glama' "...do not occur elsewhere in Icelandic, but are well evidenced in modern Norwegian and Swedish..." as 'to mock, sneer' and 'to be rowdy, talk noisily,' respectively. Note that 'glissa' can also simply mean 'to grin.'

31.6: The adjective 'gramr' ('wrathful, angry'), when found in the plural, is often used to mean 'fiends, demons' or 'enemies,' but here I think it may imply people with the potential to be 'vengeful,' i.e. those who would seek retribution for one's insults.

STANZA 32

1.) There are many souls
2.) who stand loyal at arms,
3.) yet at meals, sit and quarrel.
4.) The conflicts of man
5.) will forever remain,
6.) while tables are set for war.

ORIGINAL LANGUAGE

1.) Gu[m]nar marg[ir]
(*men - many)

2.) erusk gagnholl[ir]
(are+<to each other> - very+loyal)

3.) en at vi[r]ði [v]recas[k].
(yet - at - meal - *{contend}+<with each other>)

4.) aldar róg
(<oť> *mankind - ⸲strife)

5.) þ[at] mun æ v[er]a
(it - will - always - exist)

6.) órir gestr við gest.
([while] *argues - guest - with - guest)

NOTES

32.1: The noun 'gumi' was used in Hávamál as a poetic stand-in for 'man,' but a literal translation is 'groom.' Related to the verb 'guma' and/or 'geyma' ('to keep, watch, mind'), the original sense is one of 'caretaker,' and was used in phrases like "brúð-gumi" = "groom (i.e. caretaker) - <of the> bride" and "hús-gumi" = "groom (i.e. caretaker) - <of the> house."

32.3: The verb 'vreka' can have a range of meanings, including 'to drive (something) away, or in a specific direction,' 'to pursue (an activity, or course of action),' 'to push or throw (something)' or even '(of a weapon) to thrust.' But here, I believe it's being used as 'to push against (verbally or physically), to contend with.'

32.4: The noun 'öld' (here in genitive case as 'aldar') can have a range of possible meanings, which include 'a time, an age (of history),' 'a century, a hundred (years)' or even 'a hundred (people), many people; mankind.' Note the similarity with the Roman noun 'century' which could mean '100 years' or 'a 100-man unit of the Roman army.'

32.4: The noun 'róg' means 'a slander' or 'slandering,' but could be used in poetry to mean 'arguing' or 'strife' in general.

32.6: The verb 'óra' can have a range of meanings, including 'to speak (excessively or extravagantly), to rave,' 'to speak (excessively or extravagantly) against (someone), to argue with,' 'to speak (exaggeratedly), to trick or prank' or even 'to speculate (wildly), to guess.'

STANZA 33

1.) A morsel before,
2.) should a fellow oft have,
3.) lest happens to fare for feast.
4.) Else they sit and brood,
5.) behave as though starving,
6.) then speak and visit the least.

ORIGINAL LANGUAGE

1.) Árliga v[er]ðar
(*{beforehand} - *portion (of food))

2.) skyli m[aðr] oft fá
(should - person - often - procure)

3.) ne[m]a t[il] kyn[n]is ko[m]i.
(unless - for - *{hospitality} - come)

4.) sitr ok snóp[ir]
([else one] sits - and - pines)

5.) lætr sem sólgin[n] sé
(behaves - as if - starved - is)

6.) ok kan[n] fregna at fáu.
(and - is able - <to> inquire - about - little)

NOTES

33.1: The adverb 'árliga' typically means 'early,' but here I think it's being used in the sense of 'beforehand,' (i.e. before one arrives for the visit).

33.1: The noun 'verðr' can mean 'a meal,' 'a portion (of food),' or even 'a ration.' Here I think it's being used to imply a small portion, a snack to ensure one doesn't get hungry while visiting.

33.3: The noun 'kynni' means 'closeness, familiarity,' but can also mean 'sociability, friendliness,' or perhaps even 'hospitality.' In some contexts, it can also mean 'a social visit (to a close friend or kinsman).' Here I think it's being used to imply a visit where a meal is anticipated.

STANZA 34

1.) A rough detour, 'tis,
2.) to a stingy friend's row,
3.) though upon the path they are.
4.) While to gen'rous friend's,
5.) fine trails will often go,
6.) though the faring may be far.

ORIGINAL LANGUAGE

1.) Afhvarf mikit
(*{detour} - significant)

2.) e[r] til ills vinar
(is - to - *{stingy} - friend's)

3.) þót[t] á brautu búi.
(although - on - [the] way - <may> live)

4.) en t[il] góðs vinar
(but - to - *{generous} - friend's)

5.) lig[g]ia gagnveg[ir]
(lead - *{easy+roads})

6.) þót[t] h[ann] sé fir[r] farin[n].
(although - he - <may> be - farther - *{away})

73

NOTES

34.1: The compound 'af-hvarf' is the noun 'hvarf,' meaning 'a turning away,' and the preposition 'af,' meaning 'from.' So, 'af-hvarf' means 'a turning away from,' and is generally accepted to mean 'a turning aside' or 'deviation from the direct path'; in essence, 'a detour.'

34.2 & 4: Here we see a contrast drawn between 'ills vinar' in line two and 'góðs vinar' in line four. On the simplest level, these can mean 'bad friend' and 'good friend,' respectively. But what does this really mean? Obviously, we're not talking about 'bad' in the sense of 'evil,' but more likely in the sense of 'poor in quality.' We must also take into account that in Old Norse the adjectives 'illr' and 'góðr' were sometimes used to denote a person being 'stingy' or 'generous' as well. This was especially true when paired with the preposition 'af' or an appropriate genitive noun, such as "illr af aurum" ('stingy - with - gold') and "góðr matar" ('generous - <with> meat'); the latter of which was considered synonymous with being 'a good host.' So while we cannot be certain as to the exact intent behind the author's choice in words, it's possible that a greater wealth of meaning was implied here beyond simply 'bad' and 'good.'

34.5: The compound 'gagn-vegir' is the noun 'vegr' (in plural) meaning 'ways, roads,' paired with the prefix 'gagn-,' meaning 'straight through' or 'direct.' Though it's been variously translated as 'direct paths,' 'straight ways,' or even as 'shortcuts,' I believe the underlying implication is 'easy roads' (i.e. not difficult to traverse).

34.6: The past participle 'farinn' (from the verb 'fara' which means 'to fare') typically means 'gone,' but here I think it implies being farther 'removed' or 'away.'

STANZA 35

1.) Soon, one ought to leave,
2.) and tarry long, should not,
3.) nor stay in stead forever.
4.) The loved may be loathed
5.) if too long they remain
6.) in the rooms of some other.

ORIGINAL LANGUAGE

1.) Ganga [skal]
(go - *[should])

2.) s[ka]la gestr v[er]a
(should+not - visitor - stay)

3.) ey í einu[m] stað[.]
(forever - in - one - place)

4.) ljúfr v[er]ð[r] leið[r]
(beloved - becomes - loathed)

5.) ef lengi sitr
(if - [too] long - sits)

6.) an[n]ars fletju[m] á.
(another's - *rooms - in)

NOTES

35.1: The manuscript simply reads "Ganga s[ka]la gestr v[er]a ey...," "Go - should+not - visitor - stay - forever...," but most editors agree it should be written "Ganga [skal], s[ka]la gestr v[er]a ey...," "Go - should, - should+not - visitor - stay - forever..." with David A. H. Evans noting the absence of 'skal' in the manuscript as "...a clear instance of haplography," (i.e. an accidental omission due to the similarity of 'skal' and 'skala,' and their intended appearance one after the other).

35.3: In the manuscript, there is no full-stop (i.e. period) present at the end of line 3, though grammar implies there should be.

35.6: The word 'fletjum' is a plural form of the noun 'flet,' which means 'a set of rooms or benches.' However, when used in plural in poetry it is often meant to imply the home itself which might contain those things.

STANZA 36

1.) A home is better,
2.) though be it so humble;
3.) every house has its failing.
4.) Though you have two beasts
5.) and a badly-thatched hut,
6.) it's still better than begging.

ORIGINAL LANGUAGE

1.) Bú e[r] bet[ra]
(homestead - is - better)

2.) þót[t] lítit sé
(despite+that - little - <may> be)

3.) hal[l]r er hei[m]a hv[er]r.
(*{imperfect} - is - <of> homes - each one)

4.) þót[t] tvær geitr eigi
(despite+that - two - she-goats - <may> have)

5.) ok taugreftan sal
(and - *rope+roofed - hall)

6.) þ[at] e[r] þó bet[ra] en bón.
(it - is - nevertheless - better - than - *{charity})

NOTES

36.3: Though sometimes interpreted as 'every man is master at home,' a literal reading would simply state 'man - is - at home - every' with the word for 'master' nowhere in sight. This would paint the picture of an incomplete sentence in which the word 'master' has been assumed and then inserted.

My interpretation differs in two key ways; first, I believe the word often interpreted as the noun 'halr' ('man') may instead be the adjective 'hallr' ('leaning to one side, slanted') and second, the word often interpreted as the adverb 'heima' ('at home') may instead be the plural genitive of the noun 'heimr' ('home'). And if we alter our interpretation based on these changes, then we find a complete sentence which reads 'leaning to one side - is - <of> homes - each one.' I believe this to be a figurative way of saying 'Every home has its flaws' or is 'imperfect,' which fits quite well with the two lines that come before it.

36.5: The compound 'taug-reftan' means 'rope+roofed.' And while traditional roofing techniques varied by culture and region, in Viking-age Europe the poorest homes were typically roofed in thatch. 'Thatch' is a generic term which can be applied to almost any natural material used to cover a roof, such as straw, reeds, rushes, or stacks of grain. And while the methods for securing these roofing materials could also vary, one of the simplest techniques employed (and thus likely to be found on crude constructions) was referred to as 'roped thatch,' in which a layer of thatch was secured to a roof's framework by fastening a network of ropes over top of it. I believe this technique (or one very similar) is what the phrase 'taug-reptan' ('rope+roofed') is referring to.

36.6: The noun 'bón' can mean 'a prayer, a request' or simply 'a boon' (something to be thankful for, a benefit received). Here, I think it's being used in the sense of 'charity' or (begging for) 'charity.'

STANZA 37

1.) A home is better,
2.) though be it so humble;
3.) every house has its failing.
4.) For bleed, the heart will,
5.) in the one who must beg
6.) for the bread they'll be eating.

ORIGINAL LANGUAGE

1.) Bú er b[etra]
*(homestead - is - better)

2.) þ[ótt] l[ítit] s[é]
(despite+that - little - <may> be)

3.) h[allr] [er] h[eima] hv[err].
(*{imperfect} - is - <of> homes - each one)

4.) blóðugt e[r] hjarta
(*bloody - is - heart)

5.) þei[m] er biðja sk[al]
([in] that <one> - who - beg - must)

6.) s[ér] í mál hv[er]t matar.
(<for> oneself - during - mealtime - each - <for> *food)

NOTES

37.1-3: In the manuscript, these lines are heavily abbreviated as "Bú er b. þ. l. s. h. h. hv." because they're being reused from the previous stanza.

37.3: See usage in previous stanza for more details.

37.4: The adjective 'blóðugt' means 'bloody,' but here appears to be used figuratively to mean '(emotionally) wounded.'

37.6: The noun 'matr' (here shown in genitive case as 'matar') is sometimes translated as 'meat,' though it more properly means 'food' in a general sense and can even mean 'provisions' when used in the plural. The specific word for 'meat' in Icelandic is 'kjöt.'

STANZA 38

1.) From their own weapons,
2.) walkers afield should not
3.) go farther than one footstep.
4.) For seldom will know
5.) when the need upon road
6.) will arise for weapons kept.

ORIGINAL LANGUAGE

1.) Vápnu[m] sínu[m]
(<from> weapons - their <own>)

2.) sk[al]a m[aðr] vel[l]i á
(should+not - person - *{afield})

3.) feti ga[n]ga f[ra]mar.
([a] pace - go - farther [than])

4.) þvíat óvíst e[r] at vita
(for+it - un+certain - is - to - know)

5.) nær v[er]ð[r] á vegu[m] úti
(when - occurs - on - road - outdoors)

6.) geirs u[m] þörf guma.
*(spear - for - [the] need - [a] *man's)

81

NOTES

38.2: I believe the phrase 'velli á' ('in [the] field') is being used here in a manner similar to the Engl. adverb 'afield,' as in 'a person [traveling] afield, abroad, away-from-home.' So, it may be the equivalent to 'when traveling' or perhaps simply 'when out-of-doors.'

38.6: The phrasing here can seem a bit confusing, but I believe it comes out as "[the] need for [a] man's spear."

38.6: The noun 'gumi' was used in Hávamál as a poetic stand-in for 'man,' but a literal translation is 'groom.' Related to the verb 'guma' and/or 'geyma' ('to keep, watch, mind'), the original sense is one of 'caretaker,' and was used in phrases like "brúð-gumi" = "groom (i.e. caretaker) - <of the> bride" and "hús-gumi" = "groom (i.e. caretaker) - <of the> house."

STANZA 39

1.) I've never found one,
2.) with food, so blessed nor free,
3.) they'd ne'er accept same offered.
4.) Nor one whose riches
5.) ran quite so wide or deep,
6.) that coin was spurned from coffers.

ORIGINAL LANGUAGE

1.) Fan[n]ka ek mildan man[n]
(found+not - I - [so] *{giving} - [a] person)

2.) eð[a] s[vá] matar góðan
(or - so - <for> food - *{well-provisioned})

3.) at ei v[ær]i þig[g]ja þegit.
(that - never - would - *accept [hospitality] - offered)

4.) eð[a] sí[n]s féar
(or - <in> their - *wealth)

5.) svági [góðan]
(not+so - *[well-provisioned])

6.) at leið sé laun ef þægi.
(that - loathed - would be - *{riches} - if - received)

NOTES

39.1: The adjective 'mildr' means 'mild' or 'gentle,' but can also mean 'well-mannered' and 'courteous.' In the context of being a host, it can mean 'hospitable.' Here, I think the intended meaning is 'giving' to serve as a complement with a person being 'offered' something in line 3.

39.2: The phrase 'góðr matar' ('good <for> food') has been found in various forms across multiple sources, including on Swedish runic epitaphs (according to David A. H. Evans), where it generally follows the pattern of "mildr [...] ok matar góðr," which I interpret as "hospitable [...] and generous (or well-provisioned) with food." I believe this to be a way of saying someone is a good and generous host, or that "They have plenty of food, and they know how to share it."

39.3: The verb 'þiggia' ('to accept') was sometimes used in an elliptical manner (i.e. with a word missing, but understood to be implied), and that missing word was generally 'hospitality.' Here, it may be referring to food offered.

39.4: The noun 'fé' (seen here in genitive case as 'féar') can mean anything from 'livestock' (generally sheep or cattle) to the more general concepts of 'property' and 'wealth.'

39.5: This line is missing a needed adjective, with the sentiment after 'svági' ('not+so') either omitted by error, or intended to be implied. Words inserted by various editors include 'glöggur' ('stingy'), 'gjöfull' ('very liberal'), and 'ör' ('generous'). But I think the missing word may be 'góðr' (as 'well-provisioned'), reflecting its usage in phrasing from line 2.

39.6: The modern meaning of the noun 'laun' tends toward 'wages, salary,' but in the oldest sense it simply meant 'a reward' or 'benefit' of some kind. Here, I think it's being used to mean 'riches,' 'boons' or perhaps even 'gifts' (of money or livestock)' being received.

STANZA 40

1.) Of your own good wealth,
2.) which you have sorely gained,
3.) seek not, yourself, to deprive.
4.) Often leave for churls
5.) what for cherished was laid;
6.) little is certain in life.

ORIGINAL LANGUAGE

1.) Féar sí[n]s
(<from> *wealth - their <own>)

2.) er fe[n]git hefr
(which - gained - have)

3.) skylit m[aðr] þörf þola.
(should+not - person - deprivation - suffer)

4.) oft spar[ir] leiðu[m]
(often - saves - <.for the> loathed)

5.) þa[t]s hef[r] ljúfu[m] hugat
(that+which - have - <for the> loved - intended)

6.) mar[g]t ge[n]gr v[er]r en var[ir].
(much - goes - worse - than - [one] expects)

NOTES

40.1: The noun 'fé' (seen here in genitive as 'féar') can mean anything from 'livestock' (generally sheep or cattle) to the more general concepts of 'property' and 'wealth.'

STANZA 41

1.) Giving blades and garb,
2.) good friends should thus uplift;
3.) that gift they find most fitting.
4.) To and fro, that bless,
5.) those friends will longest bide,
6.) whilst gifts continue giving.

ORIGINAL LANGUAGE

1.) Vápnu[m] ok váðu[m]
([with] weapons - and - garments)

2.) sk[ul]u vin[ir] gleðjas[k]
(should - friends - gladden+<each other>)

3.) þ[at] er á sjálfum sýnst.
(that [gift] - which - on - them - [is] *best-suited)

4.) viðrgefendr ok endrgefender
(givers+toward - and - *givers+in return)

5.) erusk lengst vin[ir]
(are+<themselves> - longest - friends)

6.) ef þ[at] bíð[r] at v[er]ða vel.
(if - that - continues - to - proceed - well)

NOTES

41.3: The superlative 'sýnst' is derived from the adjective 'sýnn,' which means 'visible' or in a metaphorical sense 'clear, evident.' It can also mean something being 'well-suited' or 'appropriate.'

41.4: The compound 'endr-gefendr' translates literally as 're-givers' or 'givers+in return,' and I believe it's meant to imply one who reciprocates in the gift-giving process.

STANZA 42

1.) Unto their own friend,
2.) a friend, one ought to be,
3.) bestowing gift for its like.
4.) Warm laughter for mirth,
5.) should folk, the like, receive,
6.) but duplicity for lies.

ORIGINAL LANGUAGE

1.) Vin sínu[m]
(friend - <to> their <own>)

2.) sk[al] m[aðr] vi[n]r v[er]a
(should - [a] person - [a] friend - be)

3.) ok gjalda gjöf v[ið] gjöf[.]
(and - repay - gift - with - gift)

4.) hlátr v[ið] hlát[ri]
(*laughter - for - laughter)

5.) skyli hölðar taka
(should - *men - receive)

6.) en lausung v[ið] lygi.
(but - *{duplicity} - for - [a] lie)

NOTES

42.3: No full stop (i.e. period) is present at the end of line 3 in the manuscript, though sentence structure would suggest one should be.

42.4: Though some have rendered the noun 'hlátr' in this stanza as "mockery," I believe the underlying sense of the word is simply 'laughter.' And it's generally only taken to mean mockery when paired with phrasing such as 'hafa hlátr at' (literally 'have a laugh at'). Here, I think it's being used for 'friendly laughter' to contrast with the unfriendly lying in line 6.

42.5: The noun 'hölðr' was used in Hávamál as a poetic stand-in for 'man,' but it's actually a term for members of a social class of free landowners. It may also be related to, or a synonym with 'halr,' which was used in much the same way and meant 'hero' or 'person of great bravery.'

42.6: The noun 'lausung' is often simply rendered as 'lying,' but I think the more nuanced interpretation of 'duplicity' better captures the original intent as I see it. 'Duplicity' quite literally implies 'doubleness,' or the state of doing or saying one thing while thinking another. It implies showing a false or misleading front while keeping your true thoughts and intentions concealed. A concept which is explored more in depth by stanza 45.

STANZA 43

1.) Unto their own friend,
2.) a friend, one ought to be,
3.) to both them and their friend too.
4.) But a sworn foe's friend,
5.) not one fellow should seek
6.) to secure a friendship through.

ORIGINAL LANGUAGE

1.) Vin sínu[m]
(friend - <to> their <own>)

2.) sk[al] m[aðr] vinr v[er]a
(should - [a] person - [a] friend - be)

3.) þeim ok þ[es]s vin.
(<to> them - and - their - friend)

4.) en óvinar síns
*(but - enemy's - <of> their)

5.) skyli engi m[aðr]
(should - no - person)

6.) vinar vi[n]r v[er]a.
(friend, - [a] friend - be)

NOTES

43.4-6: The phrasing used in lines 4 through 6 can be a bit confusing, but I believe it comes out to "But - no - person - should - be - [a] friend - <of> their - enemy's - friend."

STANZA 44

1.) If a friend, you have,
2.) who is worthy of faith,
3.) and from them, you wish good gained,
4.) share your mind with theirs
5.) and seek fair gift exchange,
6.) range to visit, shine or rain.

ORIGINAL LANGUAGE

1.) Veiztu ef þú vin átt
(know <this>, - if - you - [a] friend - have)

2.) þan[n] er þú vel trúir
(such - that - you - well - trust)

3.) ok vil[l] þú af h[án]um gót[t] geta.
(and - wish - you - from - him - good - <to> gain)

4.) geði sk[a]ltu við þan[n] blanda
(*mind - <you> should - with - that <one> - *{share})

5.) ok gjöfu[m] skipta
(and - gifts - exchange)

6.) fara at fin[n]a oft.
(travel - to - meet - often)

NOTES

44.4: In its oldest usage, the noun 'geð' can have a range of possible meanings, which include 'the mind,' 'the senses,' and 'the faculty of judgment.' In more modern usage, the word tends to be used for 'the emotional state of mind; mood, disposition, or even passion.'

44.4: The verb 'blanda' means to 'to blend together, to mix' or 'to intermingle.' And I suspect it's being used here in the context of sharing thoughts to serve as a parallel with the notion of exchanging presents (i.e. as an equal and two-sided interaction).

STANZA 45

1.) If someone, you know,
2.) who's not worthy of faith,
3.) yet from them, you wish good gained,
4.) pleasing words, should speak,
5.) but wily thoughts, you plan,
6.) and lies repay with words feigned.

ORIGINAL LANGUAGE

1.) Ef þú át[t] an[n]an
(if - you - have - *another)

2.) þan[n]s þú illa t[rú]ir
(that <one>+who - you - poorly - trust)

3.) vildu af h[án]u[m] þó gót[t] geta.
(<you> wish - from - him - yet - good - <to> get)

4.) fagrt sk[a]ltu v[ið] þan[n] m[æ]la
(pleasingly - <you> should - for - that <one> - speak)

5.) en flát[t] hyg[g]ja
(but - *{craftily} - think)

6.) ok gjalda lausung v[ið] lygi.
(and - repay - *{duplicity} - for - [a] lie)

NOTES

45.1: Despite following stanza 44, which specifically mentions 'a friend,' I believe here the intent is 'another (associate),' or 'if you know another (person),' rather than 'another (friend),' as the word 'friend' in English implies a level of intimacy that would be at odds with the kind of distrust being spoken of here.

45.5: The adjective 'flár' (here being used in neuter gender and adverbially) is typically rendered as 'false, deceitful,' which can have negative connotations. But I think perhaps 'duplicitous' (saying one thing while thinking something else) or 'wily' (full of wiles, i.e. tricks or stratagems) more closely captures the original intent of this line as I see it.

45.6: The noun 'lausung' is often simply rendered as 'lying,' but I think the more nuanced interpretation of 'duplicity' better captures the original intent as I see it. 'Duplicity' quite literally implies 'doubleness,' or the state of doing or saying one thing while thinking another. It implies showing a false or misleading front while keeping your true thoughts and intentions concealed. A concept which is also touched upon in stanza 42.

STANZA 46

1.) And so that one, then,
2.) that's not worthy of faith,
3.) and suspicious you may find,
4.) jest with them, you might,
5.) but mind, you shan't express;
6.) repay what's given in kind.

ORIGINAL LANGUAGE

1.) Þat er en[n] of þan[n]
(this - is - once again - about - that <one>)

2.) er þú illa t[rú]ir
(who - you - poorly - trust)

3.) ok þér e[r] grunr at h[an]s geði.
(and - <for> you - is - suspicion - of - his - *{intent})

4.) hlæja s[ka]ltu v[ið] þei[m]
(laugh - <you> should - with - them)

5.) ok um hug m[æ]la
(*and yet - about - [your] thoughts - *speak+not)

6.) glík s[ku]lu gjöld gjöfum.
(similar - should [be] - repayments - <for> gifts)

97

NOTES

46.3: In its oldest usage, the noun 'geð' can have a range of possible meanings, which include 'the mind,' 'the senses,' and 'the faculty of judgment.' In more modern usage, the word tends to be used for 'the emotional state of mind; mood, disposition, or even passion.'

46.5: Though 'mæla' (as seen here) can be the infinitive form of the verb 'mæla' ('to speak'), it's generally agreed that this example is the imperative form 'mæl' paired with a negative suffix '-a,' thus making it 'speak+not.' And that 'ok,' generally taken as 'and,' is being employed here in the more rare but still acceptable usage of 'and yet.' Elsewise, it would directly contradict the message of stanza 45, which clearly states one should *not* speak their true thoughts to an untrustworthy person.

STANZA 47

1.) In fore times, when young,
2.) I journeyed without friend,
3.) and found myself wild and lost.
4.) Thought myself wealthy
5.) when another, I met;
6.) for man, mankind is solace.

ORIGINAL LANGUAGE

1.) Ungr var ek forðu[m]
(young - was - I - long ago)

2.) fór ek ein[n] saman
(traveled - I - [as] one - alone)

3.) þá varð ek villr vega[.]
(then - became - I - wild - <of> ways)

4.) auðigr þóttumk
(wealthy - thought+myself)

5.) e[r] ek an[n]an fan[n]
(when - I - another - found)

6.) m[aðr] er m[anns] gaman.
([a] person - is - [another] person's - joy)

NOTES

47.3: No full stop (i.e. period) is present at the end of line 3 in the manuscript, though sentence structure would suggest one should be.

STANZA 48

1.) When brave and giving,
2.) the greatest way, folk live,
3.) and seldom will sorrow bear.
4.) But the timid one
5.) will at all things, tremble,
6.) while the miser grieves gifts shared.

ORIGINAL LANGUAGE

1.) Mild[ir] fræknir
(*{generous} - [and] brave)

2.) m[enn] bazt lifa
(people - best - live)

3.) sjaldan sút ala.
(seldom - sorrow - bear)

4.) en ósnjallr m[aðr]
(but - *not+bold - person)

5.) ug[g]ir h[v]atvetna
(fears - anything)

6.) sýt[ir] æ gløg[g]r v[ið] gjöfu[m].
(*grieves - always - [the] stingy - at - gifts)

NOTES

48.1: The adjective 'mildr' means 'mild' or 'gentle,' but can also mean 'well-mannered' and 'courteous.' In the context of being a host, it can mean 'hospitable.' Here, I think it implies 'generous,' to serve in contrast to 'stingy' in line 6.

48.4: The adjective 'snjallr' means 'quick, fast,' but also 'quick (to understand), clever' and 'quick (to engage in), eager, bold.' So, it's often used as a term denoting one is 'wise' or 'brave.' Used in the current context and paired with a negative prefix, I believe the implication is 'cowardly.'

48.6: Here, I believe the implication is that a 'stingy [person]' will always grieve, or feel sorrow when either giving or receiving gifts. They feel sorrow in the act of giving, because they fear the loss of what they have, but they also feel sorrow in receiving, because an obligation is created which demands they give in return.

STANZA 49

1.) With garments of mine,
2.) I made gifts, while faring,
3.) for two souls, a sapling pair.
4.) Respected, they felt,
5.) once fine'ry, they sported;
6.) honored not, are those left bare.

ORIGINAL LANGUAGE

1.) Váðir mínar
(clothes - my)

2.) gaf ek velli at
(gave - I - afield)

3.) tvei[m] trém[önnu]m.
(two - *made from wood+persons)

4.) rekkar þ[at] þóttus[k]
({*respected} - thus - deemed+<themselves>)

5.) e[r] þ[ei]r rift höfðu
(when - they - *linen clothes - had)

6.) neiss er nökkviðr m[aðr] halr.
(*{not honored} - is - exposed - *person)

103

NOTES

49.1-6: I believe two layers of cultural reference can be applied here. First, the Norse story of creation, which depicts the first man and woman as made from the wood of trees by gods. After being made and given gifts of life, they were also given clothing (in Snorri's Prose Edda). Second, the Norse religious practice of carving human-like idols from wood, and then presenting them with offerings (which included clothing and meat, according to Ragnar Loðbrók's Saga).

This stanza may also be a criticism of the Christian story of creation, in which the first man and woman were left naked after being formed.

49.3: Several examples exist in Norse literature of beings dubbed 'trémaðr.' From a wooden automaton given life by the insertion of a human heart (in the story of Hakon Jarl), to a 60ft idol worshiped and consulted for advice (see Ragnar's Saga). But the phrase simply means 'made from wood+person.'

49.4: The adjective 'rekkr' means 'a straight, upright person, a franklin,' with a franklin being a free landowner from an upper social class. I believe it's used here to imply a person being 'respected.'

49.5: Linen clothes were fine garments of the upper classes.

49.6: The adjective 'neiss,' sometimes translated as 'ashamed,' was proposed to mean 'defenseless, destitute of help,' by Anne Holtsmark (Norwegian philologist). In its use here contrasting with 'rekkr' ('respected'), I think it may imply 'not honored.'

49.6: The nouns 'maðr' ('man, person') and 'halr' ('man, hero') are synonyms and may have been doubled here in error. Most editions remove one.

STANZA 50

1.) A young tree withers,
2.) when lone on open ground;
3.) guard it, bark nor needles, well.
4.) Similar the one,
5.) who no other soul loves;
6.) how long can their life prevail?

ORIGINAL LANGUAGE

1.) Hrörnar þöll
(withers - young fir-tree)

2.) sú er stendr þorpi á
(that - which - stands - *cleared land - upon)

3.) hlýrat he[nni] börkr né bar[r].
(shelters+not - *her - bark - nor - leaves)

4.) s[vá] er m[aðr]
(thus - is - person)

5.) sá er man[n]gi an[n]
(he - who - no+one - *bestows [love])

6.) hvat sk[al] h[ann] lengi lifa.
(how - shall - he - long - live)

NOTES

50.2: The noun 'þorp' is often used to mean 'a village,' but I believe its original meaning was simply 'cleared land' (i.e. a flat, open space suitable for a settlement), and that only later it came to be synonymous with settlements placed on such land. I believe the usage of the word in this stanza supports that notion, as well as the Proto-Germanic noun 'þurpa' from which it is theorized to derive (and which has a dual meaning of both 'rural settlement' and 'cleared land').

50.3: In Icelandic, the word 'þöll' ('a young fir-tree') is a feminine noun, so feminine pronouns are used to describe it. While in English, trees are generally referred to as being neuter in gender.

50.5: The verb 'unna' (here seen as 'ann' in the present tense) means 'to grant' or 'to bestow' in the oldest sense. But it was used so frequently in the phrasing of 'unna... ást' ('to bestow... love') that its meaning eventually became synonymous with 'to love.' In this line, I believe that is the meaning that's implied.

STANZA 51

1.) Fiercer than a blaze,
2.) can burn, 'tween ill-matched friends,
3.) affections, for five brief days.
4.) But then are snuffed out
5.) when the sixth day arrives,
6.) and the whole affair will fade.

ORIGINAL LANGUAGE

1.) Eldi heitari
(fire - hotter [than])

2.) bren[n]r m[eð] illu[m] vinu[m]
(burns - between - *{ill-suited} - friends)

3.) frið[r] v. daga[.]
(fellowship - *five - days)

4.) en þá sloknar
(but - then - is extinguished)

5.) er in[n] vi. ke[m]r
(when - the - *sixth - arrives)

6.) ok versnar allr vinskapr.
(and - deteriorates - whole - friendship)

NOTES

51.2: The adjective 'illr' means 'bad' or 'poor (in quality).' Here, I believe it's being used to imply friends who are 'ill-suited' for one another.

51.3: No full stop (i.e. period) is present at the end of line 3 in the manuscript, though sentence structure would suggest one should be.

51.3 & 5: The Roman numerals 'v.' (for five) and 'vi.' (for six) are used in the manuscript, rather than Icelandic words for those numbers.

STANZA 52

1.) A large gift alone,
2.) a fellow need not give;
3.) one oft gains good with little.
4.) With a loaf half-broke
5.) and a bottle half-shared,
6.) I've found new friends with mettle.

ORIGINAL LANGUAGE

1.) Mikit eit[t]
(*large <amount> - alone)

2.) sk[al]a m[ann]i gefa
(need+not - person - give)

3.) oft kaup[ir] s[ér] í litlu lof.
(often - gains - <for> self, - by - *little, - praise)

4.) m[eð] halfu[m] hleif
(with - half - loaf)

5.) ok m[eð] höllu keri
(and - with - tilted - container)

6.) fekk ek mér félaga.
(found - I - myself - [a] friend)

NOTES

52.1 & 3: The adjectives 'mikill' (here in neuter gender as 'mikit') and 'lítill' (also in neuter as 'litlu'), meaning 'large' and 'little' respectively, seem used here as substantive nouns meaning a 'large <amount>' and a 'little <amount>.'

STANZA 53

1.) For one of small ports,
2.) who plies on small waters,
3.) small is the world which they know.
4.) Thus all souls do not,
5.) the same awareness hold;
6.) only half-aware are most.

ORIGINAL LANGUAGE

1.) Lítilla sanda
(<of> small - *shores)

2.) lítilla sæva
(<of> small - seas)

3.) lítil e[r]u geð gu[m]a.
(small - are - *{perceptions} - <of> [such a] *man)

4.) því all[ir] m[enn]
(thus - all - people)

5.) v[e]rðat jafnspak[ir]
(become+not - equally+aware)

6.) halb e[r] öld h[v]ar.
(*half-[aware] - *{are} - many people - everywhere)

NOTES

53.1-3: This stanza has been interpreted in many ways by various authors. The original language, as well as the intent, is generally considered obscure, with David A. H. Evans calling it a "locus desperatus" ('a hopeless place'). So, to call this passage open to interpretation is an understatement. But I believe the unusual genitive structure of these lines might read as follows: 'Small are the perceptions <of> a man <of> small shores, [a man] <of> small seas, (i.e. a person who has only made small journeys to small places).'

53.1: The noun 'sandr' means 'sand,' but the plural form (as used here) was often used to mean 'sea-shores' or 'sandbanks.'

53.3: In its oldest usage, the noun 'geð' can have a range of possible meanings, which include 'the mind,' 'the senses,' and 'the faculty of judgment.' In more modern usage, the word tends to be used for 'the emotional state of mind; mood, disposition, or even passion.'

53.3: The noun 'gumi' was used in Hávamál as a poetic stand-in for 'man,' but a literal translation is 'groom.' Related to the verb 'guma' and/or 'geyma' ('to keep, watch, mind'), the original sense is one of 'caretaker,' and was used in phrases like "brúð-gumi" = "groom (i.e. caretaker) - <of the> bride" and "hús-gumi" = "groom (i.e. caretaker) - <of the> house."

53.6: Instead of the Icelandic adjective 'halfr,' the manuscript uses the Old High German cognate 'halb' (both meaning 'half'). Many editors replace the latter with the former, but I've chosen to preserve the original German spelling. It's an interesting example of the usage of foreign loan-words.

53.6: The noun 'öld,' literally meaning 'a hundred' or metaphorically 'many people,' is used here in the singular and is accompanied by a singular verb (i.e. 'half-[aware] - is - many people'), but the phrasing sounds better in English as a plural.

STANZA 54

1.) More informed than not,
2.) needs a fellow to be,
3.) but some things need not be known.
4.) These are the people,
5.) most pleasantly, that live,
6.) who leave some knowledge alone.

ORIGINAL LANGUAGE

1.) Meðal snotr
(moderately - knowing)

2.) skyli m[ann]a hv[err]
(should - person - every)

3.) æva t[il] snotr sé.
(not - too - knowing - be)

4.) þei[m] er[u] fyrða
(these - are - [the] *men)

5.) fegrst at lifa
(most pleasantly - that - live)

6.) er vel mar[g]t vitu[t].
(who - too - much - *know+not)

NOTES

54.1-3: I believe the subject here is the amount or type of knowledge a person possesses, and not necessarily how "wise" they are, as some have rendered it. If you follow the train of thought as it continues through the next two stanzas, the example of 'knowing too much' provided by Odin is 'örlög sín,' or knowing 'one's own fate,' i.e. the way one is fated to die. This is something Odin learned in the course of his journeys. And according to the prevailing Norse cultural view at the time, one's 'örlög' was a fixed and unchangeable thing, woven by the Norns (i.e. Fates) before one's birth.

Among other things, Odin embodies the search for knowledge and wisdom. So it can seem paradoxical that he would caution against the gaining of "too much knowledge." Yet I believe the message here is that even the god of knowledge and wisdom has found there are certain times when a thing is not worth knowing. And if we take the example cited in Hm. 56, then we can deduce that such a time was thought to be when a thing could not be changed, and when knowing about it would only cause one suffering.

54.4: The collective noun 'fyrðar' was used in Hávamál as a poetic stand-in for 'men,' but a literal translation is '(those who) travel, or gather (together), (e.g. in times of great need, or when called upon); a militia force of citizen-soldiers,' which may be related to the Norwegian verb 'ferda' = 'to travel' and the Old English noun 'ferd' = 'a journey; an army.'

54.6: David A. H. Evans notes that the insertion of a negative suffix on either the verb 'er' in line 4 (making 'era') or 'vitu' in line 6 (making 'vitut') is most likely appropriate, else lines 4-6 would seem to contradict the message of 1-3. I agree with this assertion, and have amended 'vitu' in line 6 to read as 'vitut' = "who - too - much - know+not" vs "who - too - much - know." The absence of a negative suffix in the manuscript may be a scribal error.

STANZA 55

1.) More informed than not,
2.) needs a fellow to be,
3.) but some things need not be known.
4.) A well-journeyed soul
5.) too seldom is joyful,
6.) if knowing too much, has grown.

ORIGINAL LANGUAGE

1.) Meðal snotr
*(moderately - knowing)

2.) s[kyli] m[ann]a h[verr]
(should - person - every)

3.) [æva til snotr sé].
(not - too - knowing - be)

4.) þvíat snotrs m[ann]s hjarta
(because - [a] knowing - person's - heart)

5.) v[er]ð[r] sjalda[n] glat[t]
(becomes - seldom - glad)

6.) ef sá er al[l]snotr e[r] á.
(if - that <one> - is - *too+knowing - who - has [it])

NOTES

55.1-3: The manuscript heavily abbreviates lines 1-3 as "Meðal snotr s. ma h.," because the lines are being reused from stanza 54. This was a common practice used in old manuscripts for saving page space.

55.6: The compound adjective 'al-snotr' is comprised of two elements, the prefix 'al-' and the adjective 'snotr' ('wise' or 'knowing'). The manuscript uses abbreviations freely, so it's not clear whether the prefix 'al-' or 'all-' was intended, and that distinction could make a difference in the meaning. The prefix 'al-' is used to imply that which is 'thoroughly' or 'completely' so, and might imply 'all+knowing.' While the prefix 'all-' is used as an intensifier and might simply mean 'very much+knowing.'

In either event, the shared theme of stanzas 54, 55, and 56 seems to be that of someone who 'knows too much' in the form of knowing 'one's own fate' (i.e. the way one is going to die), and so I believe the implication of 'al-snotr' in this context would be 'overly' or 'too-knowing.' In accordance with that theory, I have amended line six to read 'al[l]snotr', as the prefix 'all-' seems a more logical fit for this meaning, and may be what the original scribe intended.

STANZA 56

1.) More informed than not,
2.) needs a fellow to be,
3.) but some things need not be known.
4.) Like their doom foretold,
5.) which no fellow ought learn,
6.) so wits be free of such woe.

ORIGINAL LANGUAGE

1.) Meðal s[notr]
*(moderately - knowing)

2.) s[kyli] m[ann]a h[verr]
(should - person - every)

3.) [æva til snotr sé].
(not - too - knowing - be)

4.) örlög sín
(*fate - <of> oneself)

5.) viti e[n]gi m[aðr] fyrir
(<should> know - no - person - ahead)

6.) þei[m] er sorga lausastr sefi.
(<for> them - is - <of> *[such] worries - most free - mind)

NOTES

56.1-3: The manuscript heavily abbreviates lines 1-3 as "Meðal s. s. ma h.," because the lines are being reused from stanzas 54 and 55. This was a common practice used in old manuscripts for saving page space.

56.4: The noun 'ör-lög' means what has been "laid down" or "established" in the past (by the fates), i.e. 'pre-destiny.' In the Icelandic culture it is used to mean 'fate' or 'destiny' in a general sense, but also at times in a very specific sense of one's 'doom' (i.e. fated death).

56.6: I do not believe the implication here is that one who avoids knowledge of their own fated death will be freest of *all* worries, but rather they'll be freest of worries about *that subject* specifically. And that perhaps the hallmark of knowing 'too much' about a thing is when that knowledge increases one's worries while affording no benefit.

In the course of his journeys to gain knowledge and wisdom, Odin gained one piece of knowledge he may have deemed 'too much.' And that was the knowledge of his own fated demise. According to the Poetic and Prose Eddas, it is Odin's fate to die in battle against the wolf Fenrir at Ragnarök (i.e. the end and subsequent rebirth of the world). The myths contain examples of Odin being worried by this knowledge, and taking steps that try to prevent it (e.g. the pre-emptive binding of Fenrir, and Odin gathering forces in Valhalla to aid him in the final battle). Yet, despite these efforts, there is no evidence presented in the stories that such steps will be effective. So, perhaps in part because prevailing Norse beliefs held that fate was an unchangeable thing, Odin's knowledge of his own fated demise is held up here as an example of knowing 'too much.'

STANZA 57

1.) Wood, from blazing wood,
2.) will light and be consumed,
3.) as fire does kindle flame.
4.) And one soul, from next,
5.) grows knowing by asking,
6.) but lacking when too restrained.

ORIGINAL LANGUAGE

1.) B[ra]ndr af b[ra]ndi
(*burning wood - by means of - burning wood)

2.) bren[nr] unz brun[n]in[n] er
(burns - until - [fully] consumed - is)

3.) funi kviekisk af funa.
(flame - is kindled - by means of - flame)

4.) m[að]r af m[ann]i
(person - by means of - person)

5.) v[er]ðr at máli kuðr
(becomes - from - conversing - knowing)

6.) en t[il] dælskr af dul.
(but - too - *ignorant - from - *{reluctance})

NOTES

57.1: The noun 'brandr' can mean 'a firebrand (i.e. a piece of burning wood typically used for starting fires - the medieval equivalent of a large match),' 'a flame,' 'a burning log (in general),' or even metaphorically 'a sword' (perhaps due to the flickering, reflective appearance of the metal).

57.6: The adjective 'dælskr' is often translated as 'foolish,' but properly it means 'from, or belonging to a small dale, (i.e. a small, isolated region),' and metaphorically 'unrefined' or 'ignorant.'

57.6: The noun 'dul' properly means 'concealment,' but here I believe it's being used to mean 'concealment (of one's thoughts and feelings), reticence,' i.e. a reluctance to converse and be open. See also stanza 44, in which one is encouraged to share their 'mind' (i.e. thoughts and feelings) with a trustworthy friend.

STANZA 58

1.) They should rise early,
2.) who another's, would have,
3.) of wealth or life, the glory.
4.) Rare' the lying wolf
5.) will reap a fattened leg,
6.) nor sleeping soul, victory.

ORIGINAL LANGUAGE

1.) Ár sk[al] rí[sa]
(early - should - rise)

2.) sa er an[n]ars vill
(that <one> - who - another's - wishes)

3.) fé eð[a] fjör hafa.
(*{assets} - or - life - <to> *have)

4.) sjaldan lig[g]iandi úlfr
(seldom - lying [down] - wolf)

5.) lær u[m] getr
(thigh - around - gets [its mouth])

6.) né sofandi m[aðr] sigr.
(nor - sleeping - person - victory)

NOTES

58.3: The noun 'fé' can mean anything from 'livestock' (generally sheep or cattle) to the more general concepts of 'property' and 'wealth.'

58.3: The intent of the first three lines is somewhat open to interpretation. The Icelandic verb 'hafa' can take on a range of meanings depending on the context; it can mean 'to have', 'to win', or even 'to take.' So these lines might be saying 'Get up early (and work hard), if you wish to have the (similarly impressive) life or wealth of another.' It might also be saying 'Get up early (and gain the element of surprise), if you wish to take the (actual) life or wealth of another.'

Given the violent reputation of the Vikings, some might assume the latter meaning was intended. But we must also take into account that not all Norse people during the Viking Age were Vikings. So, the former, less violent interpretation of this stanza is a valid possibility. And if one follows the train of thought into the next stanza, which seems a direct continuation, we more clearly see a description of getting up early and working hard for one's wealth. So, I'm inclined to favor the less violent version.

STANZA 59

1.) Early, should awake,
2.) that one with meager help,
3.) and in all their efforts, strive.
4.) Much remains undone
5.) by one who sleeps past morn;
6.) much of wealth is won by drive.

ORIGINAL LANGUAGE

1.) Ár sk[al] rísa
(early - should - rise)

2.) sá er á yrkendr fá[a]
(that <one> - who - has - workers - few)

3.) ok ganga síns v[er]ka á vit.
(and - go - his - tasks - *about <doing>)

4.) mart u[m] dvelr
(many <things> - because of - ⁺remain [undone])

5.) þann er um morgin sefr
(that <one> - who - past - morning - sleeps)

6.) hálfr e[r] auðr und hvötu[m].
(*half-[gained] - is - wealth - under <the sway of> - *{initiative})

NOTES

59.3: The words "á vit" are most likely an adverbial phrase consisting of the prep. 'á' ('to, towards') paired with a truncated form of the verb 'vita' (in the sense of 'see, try'). This phrasing was sometimes used to imply going 'about' (a place), i.e. to visit, explore, or going 'about' (a task), i.e. to attempt or try (an activity).

59.4: In pre-electric, agrarian societies, the amount of time one had to perform their work was dictated by the amount of sunlight in a day. One could not simply "work late" to make up for lost time. So the act of sleeping past morning meant that a person had that much less time to complete their required tasks.

59.6: In the manuscript, the adjective phrase 'half-' is left unfinished, perhaps because the author assumed the meaning was implied. But given the general theme of both the preceding stanza and this one, I think it's safe to speculate the intent was 'half-[gained].'

59.6: There are three grammatically viable options for the word 'hvötum,' which makes this line open to interpretation. It might represent the plural dative of the noun 'hvati,' which can mean 'hurriers,' 'initiators.' It might represent the singular or plural of the adjective 'hvatr,' once again in the dative, which can mean '<the> bold', '<the> vigorous', '<the> lively.' Or, it might represent the plural dative of the noun 'hvöt,' which can mean 'instigations.'

Though all of these follow a general trend and might be suitable when describing the type of persons or the type of activities that might be prone to success, I prefer the third possibility. I believe here, the plural of the noun 'hvöt' may be utilized in a collective sense to represent '[acts of] initiative,' or simply 'initiative.'

STANZA 60

1.) From firewood, well-cured
2.) and covered against wet,
3.) one should know how much to take;
4.) and from the woodland,
5.) if long it will endure
6.) for present and future's sake.

ORIGINAL LANGUAGE

1.) Þur[r]a skíða
(*dried - firewood)

2.) ok þakin[n]a næf[ra]
(and - covered - [by] *birch bark)

3.) þ[es]s kan[n] m[aðr] mjöt~~uðr~~
(<from> that - *knows - person - *{right amount} [to take])

4.) þ[es]s viðar
([and] <from> that - woodland)

5.) e[r] vin[n]as[k] megi
(which - last - must)

mál ok mizze[ri].
([a small] portion of time - and - [many] seasons)

NOTES

60.1: Firewood is often cut, stacked, and dried months in advance (a process called 'curing' or 'seasoning'), before it is used in making fires.

60.2: Birch bark was used in many applications due to its tough, flexible, and waterproof nature, such as basket-making, lining canoes, and serving as an insulative layer beneath the sod material on a sod-roofed home. It's also feasible that sections of it may have been used to cover the tops of stacks of firewood left out in the open to dry, much as modern-day individuals will do with plastic tarps. This would be done to prevent rain from soaking into the wood, while keeping the sides open to the air for curing. Another possibility is that 'birch bark covered' may imply the firewood was stored beneath a sod roof, as birch bark was used as a waterproof, insulative layer in such constructions. In either case, I believe it implies the firewood is covered and stored.

60.3: The manuscript simply states "kann maðr," "[a] person knows," but given the advisory tone of Hávamál, I believe the intention is something closer to '[a] person [should] know' or even '[a sensible] person knows.'

60.3: The word in the manuscript is not simply 'mjöt,' as most editors present it. Instead, it is 'miotuðc,' which was perhaps intended as 'miotuðr' (making more sense). In his dictionary of Old Icelandic, under the noun 'mjöt,' Cleasby states the following about this line, "...'mjötuðr' from Vsp., the preceding poem, seems to have been in the transcriber's mind, and so he first wrote 'mjotvþc' and then dotted the 'v,' denoting that the last three letters were to be struck out."

There is a noun 'mjötuðr' in Old Icelandic, but the word is generally used to denote a god, and means 'dispenser (of fate),' or is sometimes used for 'the fate' or 'the bane' of someone or something. However, it does not seem to belong here, and the noun 'mjöt' ('measure,' 'the right measure') seems the better fit.

STANZA 61

1.) Washed clean and well-fed,
2.) one should fare to gath'ring,
3.) though garments may not be grand.
4.) Of leggings and boots,
5.) be not one aggrieved,
6.) nor of one's horse either;
7.) though plain, yet straight you should stand.

ORIGINAL LANGUAGE

1.) Þvegin[n] ok mettr
(washed - and - fed)

2.) ríði m[aðr] þingi at
(<should> ride - person - *assembly - toward)

3.) þót[t] h[ann] séð væd[d]r t[il] vel.
(although - he - <may> not+be - dressed - too - well)

4.) skúa ok bróka
(<of> shoes - and - <of> pants)

5.) skam[m]is[k] e[n]gi m[aðr]
(<should> be ashamed - no - person)

6.) né hests in heldr
(nor - <of> horse - yet - either)

7.) þót[t] h[ann] haf[it] góðan.
(although - he - <may> not+have - good [ones])

127

NOTES

61.2: A 'þing' (pronounced as 'thing') was a general assembly in early Germanic societies. A variety of activities could take place at a 'þing' ranging from simple commerce to the settlement of disputes between clans and even the election of new public officials.

STANZA 62

1.) Searches and scrounges,
2.) when arrives at the sea,
3.) an eagle o'er endless blue.
4.) And so too, the one,
5.) who among many fares
6.) and finds their defenders few.

ORIGINAL LANGUAGE

1.) Snap[ir] ok gnap[ir]
(scrounges - and - *{cranes} [its neck])

2.) e[r] t[il] sævar ke[m]r
(when - to - waters - arrives)

3.) örn á aldin[n] mar.
(*eagle - above - everlasting - sea)

4.) s[vá] er m[aðr]
(such - is - person)

5.) er m[eð] mörgu[m] ke[m]r
(when - among - many - arrives)

6.) ok á formælendr fá[a].
(and - has - *{vocal supporters} - few)

NOTES

62 & 63: In the manuscript, the text of stanza 63 appears before stanza 62. However, special markings (a forward slash followed by a dot) appear above the word 'Snap' in the second of these two stanzas which may indicate a mistake is present and they need to be reversed in order. Most editions of the text follow that indication and present them as I've done here.

62.1: The verb 'gnapa' means 'to jut out, stoop forward,' and in the context of this stanza, I take that to mean the eagle is 'craning' its neck in the act of searching for its prey.

62.3: The noun 'örn' simply means 'an eagle,' but given the context, the species 'Haliaeetus albicilla' may be implied (called 'Havørn' in Norwegian and the white-tailed or sea eagle in English).

Most birds which hunt over water, such as gulls and gannets, do so in flocks and congregate together while seeking prey. But sea eagles are large, solitary hunters which circle in the air above competing flocks of birds, often dozens of times, before swooping down to snatch prey in their talons and then retreat again. Being opportunistic hunters, the prey the sea eagle might choose is not limited to fish, they may also capture smaller birds from competing flocks who have wandered from their group, or feed on carcasses leftover by other hunters.

So, I believe the point of this metaphor is that the sea eagle is a solitary hunter, who must search and scrounge to satisfy its needs from the leavings of the larger flocks of competing birds, and that a person who has few supporters (i.e. no flock) will find themselves behaving in much the same way.

62.6: The noun 'formælandi' is a compound comprised of three elements; the prefix 'for-' meaning 'before (others)', the verb 'mæla' meaning 'to speak', and the suffix '-andi', which in this case denotes the verb is being used as a noun (i.e. '-er'). What this amounts to is 'speaker+before (others)' (often in defense of someone), a spokesperson, a vocal supporter.

STANZA 63

1.) Find and voice gossip,
2.) shall every clever fool
3.) who feels the need to know all.
4.) So only one should hear,
5.) but have a second not;
6.) nations know, if three recall.

ORIGINAL LANGUAGE

1.) Fregna ok segja
(*hear [gossip] - and - repeat)

2.) sk[al] fróðra hv[err]
(shall - *clever [fool] - every)

3.) sá er vil[l] heitin[n] horskr.
(that <one> - who - wishes - to be called - *in-the-know)

4.) ein[n] vita
(one [other] - <should> know)

5.) né an[n]ar[r] sk[al]
(not - another - should)

6.) þjóð veit ef þrír [e]ru.
([a] nation - is aware - if - three - are)

NOTES

62 & 63: In the manuscript, the text of stanza 63 appears before stanza 62. However, special markings (a forward slash followed by a dot) appear above the word 'Snap' in the second of these two stanzas which may indicate a mistake is present and they need to be reversed in order. Most editions of the text follow that indication and present them as I've done here.

62.1: The manuscript does not specify what is being heard and repeated by the listener, presumably because the composer assumed the audience could discern that from context. Yet if one takes this stanza by itself, the scope of interpretation could be very wide. However, both stanzas 28 and 62 share similar phrasing in "fregna... ok segja," "hear... and repeat," and with stanza 28 the subject is clearly cited as something that "passes between people," and is not deemed special at all (which I believe to mean gossip). These two stanzas also share a similar focus on the difficulty of keeping something a secret once it's been shared amongst multiple people. Because of these shared elements, I believe the subject here is also gossip.

62.2: The adjective 'fróðr' can have a range of meanings, which include 'educated (in a formal sense),' 'clever (in a positive sense), having quick intelligence,' 'skillful,' or even 'clever (in a negative sense), deeming oneself clever or skillful (while not truly being so); deeming oneself superior (while not truly being so).'

62.3: The adjective 'horskr' is typically used in the sense of being 'wise,' but I believe the intended meaning here is more nuanced, and that a more fitting interpretation would be 'in-the-know,' i.e. possessing inside, secret, or special knowledge.

STANZA 64

1.) One's own might and will,
2.) every wise soul ought wield
3.) with eye t'ward being modest.
4.) As one may soon find,
5.) when among fierce, they go,
6.) alone, no one is strongest.

ORIGINAL LANGUAGE

1.) Ríki sit[t]
(*power - their <own>)

2.) skyli ráðsnot[ra]
(should - <of> opinion+wise <person>)

3.) hv[err] í hófi hafa.
(each - in - moderation - wield)

4.) þá h[ann] þ[at] fin[n]r
(at that time - he - this - discovers)

5.) e[r] m[eð] fræknu[m] ke[m]r
(when - among - <the> *bold - arrives)

6.) at e[n]gi er ein[n]a hvatastr.
(that - no one - is, - *[when] alone, - <the> mightiest)

NOTES

64.1: The noun 'ríki' can mean 'power, might' in a general sense, but also 'the rule of law' and 'authority' in a more specific sense, and can even be used to mean 'a kingdom' or 'a sovereign state.' I think here it's being used to signify the exercise of one's personal will and physical power.

64.5: The adjective 'fræknum' = 'the bold' or 'the vigorous.' If the underlying meaning of this stanza ties in with stanza 62, then 'the bold' may be referring to the groups of competing hunter birds that our eagle would find itself pitted against in its quest for prey, as well as to 'the many' (people / warriors) that a person arriving at public assembly might encounter.

64.6: Though other interpretations are possible (such as 'no - single <person> - is - <the> mightiest'), I believe the meaning of this stanza ties in with that of stanza 62, and conveys the message that 'no one - is - <the> mightiest, - [when] alone' or perhaps that 'no one - is - <at their> strongest, - [when] alone.' The sea eagle in stanza 62 would, for all intents and purposes, be considered 'the king' of the skies. As one of the largest and most powerful avian predators, it would be a force to be reckoned with. Yet nature shows us that, when hunting, the sea eagle defers to the large groups of smaller, less powerful hunter birds, and chooses to keep its distance, exercising its power with reserve. Even though it may be considered 'the mightiest,' it's still wise enough to know that numbers can overwhelm.

STANZA 65

1.) One's own might and will,
2.) every wise soul ought wield
3.) with eye t'ward being reserved.
4.) For things that we say
5.) are so often repaid,
6.) each word returned and deserved.

ORIGINAL LANGUAGE

1.) [Ríki sitt]
*(power - their <own>)

2.) [skyli ráðsnotra]
(should - <of> opinion+wise <person>)

3.) [hverr í hófi hafa.]
(each - in - moderation - wield)

4.) Orða þ[ei]ra
(⁺words - those)

5.) e[r] m[aðr] öðru[m] seg[ir]
(which - person - <to> others - says)

6.) opt h[ann] gjöld u[m] getr.
(often - he - repayment - for - gets)

NOTES

65.1-3: In the manuscript, the first 3 lines of this stanza appear to be omitted. It's my theory that a scribal error is present, and that the first 3 lines of the previous stanza were intended to preface this stanza as well. We've seen this practice before of re-using the same introductory lines in more than one stanza, such as those lines found in stanzas 36 and 37, as well as 54, 55, and 56. This is typically reflected in the manuscript by writing out the same lines again, only in drastically abbreviated form, with little more than the first letter of each word followed by a period. It's possible that if the same practice was intended for this stanza, those drastically abbreviated lines may have been omitted by accident. However, there is also the possibility that three entirely unique lines were originally used to preface this stanza, and by some mishap they were lost.

65.4: The word 'orða' ('words') is capitalized in the manuscript, which normally only occurs at the start of a new stanza.

STANZA 66

1.) Too early, by far,
2.) I fared to some places,
3.) or too late, by far, they'd claim.
4.) The ale was all drunk,
5.) or draught-kegs unready,
6.) the unloved rare' hits the right day.

ORIGINAL LANGUAGE

1.) Mikilsti snem[m]a
(far too - early)

2.) ko[m] ek í marga staði
(arrived - I - in - many - [a] place)

3.) en t[il] síð í suma.
(but - too - late - in - some)

4.) öl var drukkit
(ale - was - [already] drunk)

5.) su[m]t v[ar] ólagat
(some - was - *not+{ready} [for serving])

6.) sjaldan hitt[ir] leiðr í lið.
(seldom - *hits - [the] disliked - at - *[the] best time)

NOTES

66.1-6: The gist here seems to be that the visitor in question is a disliked person (or at least considered undesirable), and when they come to homes, they are not offered hospitality. Hosts give an excuse for not offering a drink, whereupon the potential guest is told ale cannot be offered because none is available; either due to the ale having been depleted, or new ale not yet being ready to serve. Thus, the visitor laments that the undesirable rarely seems to visit places at "the right time."

66.5: The adjective 'ólagat' is the verb 'laga' in past participle form with a negative prefix. Some translators render this as 'unbrewed,' most likely due to the Cleasby / Vigfusson Icelandic-English Dictionary listing it as 'unmixed' (which could imply the brewing ingredients are not yet mixed). However, the verb 'laga' simply means 'to flow freely,' so I think 'ólagat' may imply the ale in question is 'not able to flow freely' for whatever the reason may be. And I think another strong possibility is the ale casks have not yet been vented and tapped. Before serving the contents of a wooden cask of ale, a process taking up to 48 hours must occur first, which includes setting the cask on its side in the serving position, allowing the sediment to settle to the bottom, venting the bung to allow excess carbonation to escape, and finally tapping the cask with a spigot. So, if a cask has not yet undergone this process, it could be a full two days before its contents are ready to serve. Thus making it a fine excuse if a host wishes to claim a visitor has arrived "too early" to be offered a drink.

66.6: The verb 'hitta' can mean 'to hit' or 'to visit,' much the same as we say in modern English "Let's hit the store!"

66.6: The noun 'liðr' has a literal meaning of 'joint (of the body),' but a metaphorical meaning of 'the right or best spot (for doing something); the right or best time,' as derived from the joints of a body being the most optimal places to chop when dismembering a carcass, [per David A. H. Evans].

STANZA 67

1.) In this place or that,
2.) they might invite me back,
3.) if at meals, I take no meat;
4.) or if two, I hang,
5.) at the trusted friend's home,
6.) whereon one ham, I do eat.

ORIGINAL LANGUAGE

1.) Hér ok hvar
(here - and - there)

2.) m[yn]di m[ér] hei[m] uf boðit
([they] might have - me - *{roof} - under - invited)

3.) ef þyrftak at málungi mat.
(if - wanted+not+I - at - any+mealtimes - meat)

4.) eða tvau lær hengi
(or - two - *thighs/hams - hang up)

5.) at ins tryg[g]va vinar
(at - the - *trusted - friend's)

6.) þars ek hafða eit[t] etið.
(there+where - I - have - one - eaten)

NOTES

67.2: Rather than the more standard Icelandic preposition 'of' (meaning 'of' or 'for') the word used in the manuscript appears to be 'uf,' which may be the Gothic preposition meaning 'under (going beneath).' If so, the phrase 'heim uf boðit' ('invited under abode') may be used in a manner similar to the modern English 'invited under one's roof.' Note however, that 'heim' does not normally mean 'roof,' but rather 'home' or 'abode.' It's also possible 'uf' could be a non-standard spelling of the preposition 'of,' and if so, may simply imply 'invited for home.'

67.4: The noun 'lær' means 'the thigh; a ham (of meat).'

67.5: Spelled 'trygva' in the manuscript, this might be the verb 'tryg[g]va', meaning 'to secure, to make firm and trusty.' But I think it more likely that it's the adjective 'trygga' (in a possible misspelling), meaning 'trusty, faithful,' as that seems to fit the context and sentence structure better. But I have left the original spelling intact for posterity.

STANZA 68

1.) A warm fire is best,
2.) among the brood of man,
3.) and deeds done in light of day.
4.) Wellness of body,
5.) if it be within might,
6.) and a life lived without shame.

ORIGINAL LANGUAGE

1.) Eldr e[r] beztr
(fire - is - best)

2.) m[eð] ýta sonu[m]
(among - <of> *men - sons)

3.) ok sólar sýn.
(and - <of> *sun - sight)

4.) heilyndi sit[t]
(health - one's <own>)

5.) ef m[aðr] hafa náir
(if - person - <to> keep - is able)

6.) án við löst at lifa.
([and] without - *at+fault - to - live)

NOTES

68.2: The phrase 'ýtar synir,' if translated literally, reads as '[the] sons - <of> voyagers' (from the verb 'ýta' meaning 'to launch, start on a voyage'). According to the Icelandic dictionaries of Cleasby / Vigfusson and Zoëga, it's a poetic turn-of-phrase meant to imply 'the sons of men,' (i.e. 'people' or 'humanity' in general).

68.3: The line 'ok sólar sýn' is open to interpretation. It could simply mean that 'the sight of the sun' is good for one's health. But I think it holds more depth than that.

I think a direct correlation is implied between the fire (or the warmth of fire) from line 1, and being able to maintain one's health, as mentioned in line 4. Fire can yield all sorts of benefits for the health of people, particularly in frigid northern climates. So it makes sense to me that a similar correlation might exist between 'the sight of the sun' from line 3 and living 'without (being) at fault,' i.e. 'without (being) worthy of reproach,' as mentioned in line 6.

In Hávamál 82, it is said, "...in the dark, talk with a lass: many are the eyes of day," [Benjamin Thorpe translation]. So even in ancient times, the concept of hiding certain acts under cover of darkness was well-known. If we take 'sólar sýn' to express the sentiment of '(to act in) the light of day,' rather than the more literal interpretation, then it provides a means for *how* to live 'without (being) at fault,' i.e. 'without (being) worthy of reproach,' just as the proper utilization of fire can help one to maintain their health.

I believe 'sólar sýn' is being used here to denote that one's actions should be conducted 'out in the open' or 'without concealment' in order to live 'without (being) worthy of reproach.'

68.6: I believe the prepositional phrase 'við löst' is being used here as an adjective to mean '(being) with, or at fault,' i.e. '(being) worthy of reproach.'

STANZA 69

1.) No one is unblessed,
2.) though infirm, they may be;
3.) many are blessed in children,
4.) some are blessed in friends,
5.) for others, ample wealth,
6.) while for some in deeds well-done.

ORIGINAL LANGUAGE

1.) Erat m[aðr] alls vesall
(is+not - person - wholly - *deprived)

2.) þót[t] h[ann] sé illa heill
(even though - he - <may> be - poorly - *sound)

3.) sumr er[u] af sonu[m] sæll.
(some - are - from - sons - blessed)

4.) su[m]r af frændu[m]
(some - from - *{friends and kin})

5.) su[m]r af fé ærnu
(some - from - *wealth - ample)

6.) su[m]r af v[er]kum vel.
(some - from - deeds - *well [done/known])

NOTES

69.1: The adjective 'vesall' can mean 'miserable' or 'destitute,' but in its oldest sense, it simply means 'deprived of.' And here, I think it implies 'deprived of (blessings, or reasons to live),' as evidenced by the lines which follow and attempt to illustrate the many blessings a person may yet have.

69.2: The adj. 'heill' can mean 'healthy' in a very direct and simple sense. But in its oldest usage, it's a more inclusive concept of being 'free from injury, defect, or disease' and means something closer to 'whole,' 'hale,' or 'sound' (e.g. being sound in mind and body). Given the direct mention of various physical disabilities in stanza 71, I believe the concept of 'illa heill' ('poorly - sound') used here is meant to convey 'infirmity' in a general sense that is inclusive of both illness and disability.

69.4: The masculine noun 'frændi' (here shown as 'frændum' in the plural dative) means 'loved <one>,' from the verb 'frjá' ('to love'), but implied platonic love and was used to mean 'a friend' or 'a (close) male kinsman, (e.g. cousin, uncle, nephew, etc.),' but not a brother, direct ancestor, or son, for whom other terms were used.

69.5: The noun 'fé' can mean anything from 'livestock' (generally sheep or cattle) to the more general concepts of 'property' and 'wealth.'

69.6: The phrase 'verkum vel' appears to be the plural dative of the noun 'verk' ('deeds' or 'works') followed by the adverb 'vel' ('well'). So, I can only assume that a verb of some kind is implied by the presence of 'vel,' though not explicitly stated. It might mean 'deeds - well [done],' or perhaps 'deeds - well [known],' but really, we can only guess based upon the context.

STANZA 70

1.) Living is better
2.) and being well-content;
3.) one can always catch a cow.
4.) I've seen warm fire blaze
5.) before the well-blessed soul,
6.) while death at door, froze without.

ORIGINAL LANGUAGE

1.) Bet[ra] er lifðu[m]
(better - that - <we> lived)

2.) ok sæl lifðu[m]
*(and - content - <we> remained)

3.) ey getr kvikr kú.
(always - [can] get - [the] living - [a] *cow)

4.) eld sá ek up[p] bren[n]a
(fire - saw - I - upward - *blaze)

5.) auð[u]gu[m] m[ann]i f[yrir]
(*{enriched} - man - before)

6.) en úti var dauð[i] f[yr] duru[m].
(when - outside - was - *death - before - doors)

NOTES

70.2: In the manuscript, the line reads 'ok sæl lifðu[m]' ('and - content - <we> remained'), but in 1818, Rasmus Rask proposed amending this line to 'en sé ólifðum' ('than - perhaps - <we> not+lived') and most editors have followed suit. I have chosen to stick with the original wording.

70.3: The noun 'kú' means 'a cow.' However, in ancient Iceland, cows (and livestock in general - see the noun 'fé') were representative of wealth. I believe the concept here of 'catching a cow' is being used metaphorically for 'seizing an opportunity.'

70.4: The meaning here of 'upp brenna' ('up - burn') is not entirely clear, and has been interpreted a number of different ways. It could mean 'burn - up' as in 'to consume by flame' (which some apply to the man himself, and some to his property). It could also mean 'burn - upward' as in 'to blaze' or even 'heat - up' as in 'to warm.' This meaning makes the most sense to me; i.e. a warm fire blazes before a well-blessed man, with both his fire and shelter representing the fruit of those blessings which protect him from the cold and death outside.

70.5: I believe 'auðugum' (normally 'wealthy') is being used in a figurative sense for a person who has been enriched (see root verb 'auðga,' which means 'to enrich') by blessings.

70.6: In the manuscript, the abbreviation used is 'dauð,' which some interpret as 'dauðr' (an adjective meaning 'dead') and some as 'dauði' (a noun meaning 'death'). The grammar works either way, and thus we get a variety of interpretations. David A. H. Evans, however, makes a compelling argument for the interpretation of 'death' being outside the door, and I tend to agree. In the frigid climes of ancient Scandinavia, a warm fire often meant the difference between life and death. So it's appropriate that 'death' is waiting just outside (in the cold) beyond the reach of the life-giving fire.

STANZA 71

1.) The lame can ride horse,
2.) and the handless, guide herd,
3.) while help a great deal, the deaf.
4.) For blind is better
5.) than lifeless on a pyre;
6.) nothing good is gained from death.

ORIGINAL LANGUAGE

1.) Haltr ríðr h[ros]si
([the] lame - rides - horse)

2.) hjörð rekr hundar vanr
(herd - drives - <of> hand + [the] lacking)

3.) daufr vegr ok dug[ir].
([the] deaf - *carries - and - helps)

4.) blindr e[r] bet[ri]
(blind - is - better)

5.) en bren[n]dr sé
(than - *burned - <perhaps> [to] be)

6.) nýtr ma[n]ngi nás.
(benefits - no one - <from> [a] corpse)

NOTES

71.3: This line is open to interpretation. The verb 'vega' has two distinct meanings, each theorized as deriving from a separate Proto-Germanic root; 'to lift, carry, move' [from the Proto-Germ. verb 'wegana'], and 'to attack (with a weapon),' 'to kill' [from the Proto-Germ. verb 'wigana']. While the second verb in this line, 'duga,' can also have a range of meanings, including 'to help' and 'to show prowess.'

Some interpret this line to mean 'fight and show prowess (in battle),' while I tend to favor 'carry and help.' Though either interpretation can be valid.

71.5: In ancient Norse society, the preferred method for disposing of bodies was to burn them on a funeral pyre. Though, apparently, not so in Iceland, where this text originates - due to issues early settlers may have experienced with the scarcity of trees. In his edition of Hávamál, David A. H. Evans notes that this may point to a non-Icelandic origin for these lines.

STANZA 72

1.) A child is better,
2.) even born late in life,
3.) or after a father's gone.
4.) For rarely are stones
5.) stood next to a roadside,
6.) lest raised by family for one.

ORIGINAL LANGUAGE

1.) Sonr e[r] bet[ri]
([a] son - is - better)

2.) þót[t] sé sið of alin[n]
(though - <may> be - late - for [you] - born)

3.) eft[ir] gengin[n] gu[m]a.
([or] after - *gone - [the] *man)

4.) sjaldan bautarsteinar
(seldom - *memorial stones)

5.) standa brautu at er
(stand - road - *by - that)

6.) ne[m]a reisi nið[r] at nið.
(unless - raises - relation - for - relation)

NOTES

72.1: Though the word used is 'sonr' ('a son'), this may have been done for alliterative purposes in the original poem, as the remainder of the verse can easily apply to any child, [e.g. 'a child is better (than no child)' is similar to 'living is better (than not living)' from stanza 70].

72.3: 'Genginn' is a past participle of the verb 'ganga' ('to go, walk'), and can mean 'gone' or 'departed.' But whether this is meant to imply the individual has actually died or simply departed in a more conventional manner is unclear. Perhaps it is meant to imply either.

72.3: The noun 'gumi' was used in Hávamál as a poetic stand-in for 'man,' but a literal translation is 'groom.' Related to the verb 'guma' and/or 'geyma' ('to keep, watch, mind'), the original sense is one of 'caretaker,' and was used in phrases like "brúð-gumi" = "groom (i.e. caretaker) - <of the> bride" and "hús-gumi" = "groom (i.e. caretaker) - <of the> house."

72.4: The 'bautasteinn' ('beaten' or 'road' stones, depending on the word origin you subscribe to) were carved memorial stones (perhaps 'beaten' by chisel and hammer) placed beside a public road and used to commemorate an individual who was usually dead but sometimes still living.

72.5: The last part of this line is typically rendered by editors as 'nær' ('near'), but to my eyes, the manuscript appears to read 'at,er' ('by that') instead, with the two words grouped so tightly as to be almost taken as one. This section may contain a scribal error, as the 'at' portion is written darkly and clearly, while the latter 'er' portion is written more faintly and squeezed in at the end of the line, with what may be a comma separating the two. Note that typically, the only punctuation found in the manuscript is that of periods at the mid-break and end of each stanza, so if this is a comma, the usage would be unusual.

STANZA 73

1.) Two are the takers of one.
2.) A wagging tongue will be a noose.
3.) 'Neath every hooded figure,
4.) good sense expects a ruse.

ORIGINAL LANGUAGE

1.) Tveir ro eins h[er]jar[.]
(two - are - <of> one - plunderers)

2.) tu[n]ga e[r] höf[u]ðs bani[.]
(tongue - is - <of> head - *death/ruin)

3.) e[r] m[ér] í heðin hv[er]n
(is - <for> me - in - *hooded cloak - every)

4.) handar væni.
([a] *hand - [I] expect)

NOTES

73 & 74: Though typically separated as two stanzas (likely due to overall length and the midpoint shift in subject matter), the text of stanzas 73 and 74 is actually formatted in the manuscript as a single, overlong stanza. A period appears at the end of line 73.4, but when line 74.1 begins, it does so with a lowercase letter, not an uppercase, which normally implies the text which follows belongs to the preceding stanza. Whether this formatting was intentional or a scribal error is open for debate. But regardless, most scholars agree the text of these two stanzas is unlikely to be an organic part of the surrounding poem, due to the drastic changes in both narrative style and meter. It's been theorized these lines were inserted mid-poem by a scribe or copyist who could simply find no better place to put them. They appear to be a listing of separate, but similarly-themed adages, with meanings that are sometimes obscure.

73.1-4: In the manuscript, only a single full stop (i.e. period) is present at the end of this stanza, though sentence structure suggests three should be present. And while these are seemingly separate statements, all three share the themes of wariness and danger.

73.2: The noun 'bani' means 'bane,' which can imply 'death (natural or violent - but properly violent),' 'ruin,' or even 'destruction' or 'undoing' in a more general sense.

73.3: A 'héðinn' was a short, hooded garment, sleeveless and often made of animal hide or fur, which pulled over the head; similar to a long medieval cowl or hooded poncho.

73.4: The noun 'hönd' simply means 'hand' or 'the arm and hand.' But if the themes of wariness and danger from the first two statements carry over here, then we can assume this 'hand' is one that seeks to harm or manipulate one.

STANZA 74

1.) Long nights will not dismay
2.) the one whose stocks meet need.
3.) Short are the stores of a ship,
4.) but varies the autumn eve.
5.) Conditions can change much
6.) over five short days,
7.) but more as a month does leave.

ORIGINAL LANGUAGE

1.) nót[t] v[er]ð[r] fegin[n]
(night - becomes - joyful)

2.) sá e[r] nesti t[rú]ir[.]
(that \<one\> - who - [in] provisions - has confidence)

3.) skam[m]ar ro skips rá[a]r
(short - are - \<of\> ship - [the] *nooks)

4.) hv[er]f e[r] haust g[rí]ma[.]
(variable - is - *autumn - *night)

5.) fjöld u[m] viðr[ir]
(much - over - *blows/changes)

6.) á fim[m] dögu[m]
(during - five - days)

7.) en meira á mánuði.
(but - more - during - month)

NOTES

73 & 74: Though typically separated as two stanzas, the text of stanzas 73 and 74 is actually formatted in the manuscript as a single, overlong stanza. (See 73 for full notes.)

74.1-7: In the manuscript, only a single full stop (i.e. period) is present at the end of this stanza, though sentence structure suggests three should be present. And while these are seemingly separate statements, all three share the themes of preparedness and changing conditions.

74.3: If we assume a Viking longship (though there were many ship types among their people), its storage would be quite limited. Longships were built to be narrow and light war vessels. But longships had a deck of loose, removable planks, below which was room for storage in the front and back ends, while the center space was filled with stones for ballast. As they had symmetrical ends (i.e. both front and back were pointed), these may be the 'nooks' referred to, while 'short' may refer to the length of these spaces compared to the rest of the ship.

74.4: The noun 'haust' means 'harvest,' and may be short for 'Haustmánuður,' the last month of summer in the Old Norse calendar. The ancient Norse recognized two seasons, winter and summer (each lasting six months), so their calendar did not have an autumn like the modern. 'Haustmánuður,' taking place from mid Sept. to mid Oct., could be considered an equivalent, during which the hours of sunlight would start reducing.

74.4: The noun 'gríma' means 'hood,' but was used in metaphors to mean 'the night.'

74.5: The verb 'viðra' seems no longer used in modern Icelandic. It's perhaps related to the noun 'veðr,' which means 'the weather; the wind or air,' with the verb used to denote the current state or changes in such, (e.g. 'to blow (over), to change' or 'to blow (through), to be').

STANZA 75

1.) May not be aware,
2.) the one who little knows,
3.) most become, in wrath, a fool.
4.) One soul is wealthy,
5.) while another is not;
6.) none should curse the other cruel'.

ORIGINAL LANGUAGE

1.) Veita hin[n]
(knows+not - that <person>)

2.) e[r] væt[t]ki veit
(who - nothing - knows)

3.) margr v[er]ðr af löðru[m] api.
(many - become - from - *{fear/anger} - [a] *{fool})

4.) m[aðr] e[r] auðigr
([one] person - is - wealthy)

5.) an[n]ar[r] óauðigr
(another - not+wealthy)

6.) skylit þan[n] vitka vá[a]r.
(should+not - the other - *{curse} - <with> *misfortune)

NOTES

75.3: 'Löðrum,' seemingly a plural dative noun with no known precedent, is often replaced with 'aurum' ('moist earth or mud,' taken metaphorically as 'earthly things'). A practice which began with N. F. S. Grundtvig in the 1800's and has continued since. But I think it may be a misspelling of the collective noun 'löðr' ('froth, foam'), which is properly 'löðri' in its dative form. This word's usage in compounds suggests it may have a metaphorical meaning of 'an unreasoning lather or state of agitation' (see 'löðr-mannligr' = 'cowardly; despicable' and 'löðr-menni' = 'coward; feeble person'). If so, it may mean 'an unreasoning lather (due to fear or anger)' in this context.

75.3: The noun 'api' means 'an ape,' but was used metaphorically to mean 'a fool.'

75.6: Spelled as 'vítca' (i.e. 'vítka') with a long 'i' in the manuscript, but possibly a misspelling of 'vitka' with a short vowel. If truly 'vítka' with a long 'i,' then the word makes no other known appearance in the literature (according to David A. H. Evans in his 1986 edition of Hávamál) and its meaning has only been guessed at (e.g. it's theorized as meaning 'to blame,' based on the similar verb 'víta,' which means 'to fine; reprimand'). However, the known and recorded verb 'vitka' with a short vowel means 'to bewitch,' and 'vítka' may simply be a misspelling of that word used in a metaphorical (or literal) sense as 'to curse.'

75.6: The noun 'vá' (seen here in genitive case as 'váar') means 'woe, misfortune.' And its usage here is open to interpretation. It could mean '[the poor person] should not curse [the rich person] <for the> misfortune [of being poor],' but I tend to favor a meaning of '[neither person] should curse the other <with> misfortune,' as resentment has often been known to flow freely in both directions between socioeconomic classes.

STANZA 76

1.) Livestock surely dies,
2.) and loved ones die as well;
3.) so, oneself will die the same.
4.) But words of renown
5.) never will pass from earth,
6.) for the ones who earn great fame.

ORIGINAL LANGUAGE

1.) Deyr fé
(dies - *livestock)

2.) deyja frændr
(die - *loved <ones>)

3.) deyr sjalfr it sama.
(dies - oneself - the - same)

4.) en or[ð]stír[r]
(but - *<of> reputation+fame)

5.) deyr aldregi
(dies - never)

6.) hvei[m] er sér góðan getr.
(who+ever - <for> themselves - *{great} [renown] - earns)

NOTES

76.1: The noun 'fé' can mean anything from 'livestock' (generally sheep or cattle) to the more general concepts of 'property' and 'wealth.'

76.2: The masculine noun 'frændi' means 'loved <one>,' from the verb 'frjá' ('to love'), but implied platonic love and was used to mean 'a friend' or 'a (close) male kinsman, (e.g. cousin, uncle, nephew, etc.),' but not a brother, direct ancestor, or son, for whom other terms were used.

76.4: The word 'orðs' properly means 'words,' but in some contexts it could be used to indicate 'words (about one),' i.e. 'one's reputation,' and when paired with the noun 'tírr' ('fame'), it can form a compound meaning 'the fame of one's reputation.'

76.6: Common sense tells us that both good and ill reputations can outlive those who earn them. So although the adjective 'góður' ('good') is used here, I do not think it implies the earning of 'good' (in quality) renown, but rather a 'good' (amount) of renown, i.e. significant renown, regardless of its nature.

STANZA 77

1.) Livestock surely dies,
2.) and loved ones die as well;
3.) so, oneself will die the same.
4.) But one thing I know
5.) never will pass from earth;
6.) the judgment on each one's name.

ORIGINAL LANGUAGE

1.) Deyr fé
(dies - *livestock)

2.) d[eyja] f[rændr]
*(die - *loved <ones>)

3.) [deyr sjalfr it sama].
(dies - oneself - the - same)

4.) ek veit ein[n]
(I - know - one [thing])

5.) at aldri deyr
(that - never - dies)

6.) dó[m]r u[m] dauðan hv[er]n.
(*[public] opinion - of - dead <person> - each)

159

NOTES

77.1: The noun 'fé' can mean anything from 'livestock' (generally sheep or cattle) to the more general concepts of 'property' and 'wealth.'

77.2-3: Lines 2 & 3 are abbreviated in the manuscript as "d. f. ~," but more fully spelled out when used in the preceding stanza.

77.2: The masculine noun 'frændi' means 'loved <one>,' from the verb 'frjá' ('to love'), but implied platonic love and was used to mean 'a friend' or 'a (close) male kinsman, (e.g. cousin, uncle, nephew, etc.),' but not a brother, direct ancestor, or son, for whom other terms were used.

77.6: The noun 'dómr' is a nuanced word which can be interpreted many ways. At its core, I believe it means "the fate that is placed upon one (by others or outside forces)," [theoretically from Proto-Indo-Eur. *'dʰóhₗmos' = 'that which is put, placed']. But in legal contexts, it could also mean "a judgment, or sentence," even "a court of judgment, the body of judges, or the 'court' itself." However, in a more general sense, it could take on the meaning of "judgment, estimation, or opinion (particularly as 'public opinion')," and I believe it's that shade of meaning we see used here. If stanza 76 is saying that 'significant fame' (of any kind) never dies, then stanza 77 may be saying that people's judgment about how that fame was won also never dies. In other words, fame can just as easily become infamy, so be careful what you wish for.

STANZA 78

1.) Once, were full grain halls
2.) in hands of the Fitjungs;
3.) now, a beggar's stick, they bear.
4.) E'er it is, with boons,
5.) like a blink of the eye;
6.) no friend more fickle, is there.

ORIGINAL LANGUAGE

1.) Fullar grind[r]
(full - store houses)

2.) sá ek f[yr] Fitjungs sonu[m]
(saw - I - before - <of> *Fitjungar - sons)

3.) nú b[er]a þ[ei]r vánar völ.
(now - bear - they - <of> *hope [for alms] - staff)

4.) svá e[r] auð[r]
(such - is - wealth)

5.) sem augabragð
(like - <of> *[the] eye + sudden shift)

6.) h[ann] er valtastr vina.
(he - is - most unreliable - <of> friends)

NOTES

78.2: The meaning of 'Fitjungs sonum,' 'sons of Fitjung (or Fitjungar),' is uncertain. Though theories have been proposed. Henry Adam Bellows put forward that 'Fitjung' might mean "Nourisher" and was another name for 'Jörð,' the Norse goddess of the earth. He may have derived this meaning from the noun 'fita' ('fat, grease') or the verb 'fitna' ('to become fat').

Another theory was put forward by Magnus Olsen, which was later detailed in the commentaries of David A. H. Evans in his edition of Hávamál. This theory revolves around the aftermath of the Battle of Fitjar (in 961), an event described in Hákonarmál which involved the invasion of Fitjar (on the island of Stord, in Norway) by the sons of Eric Bloodaxe. Olsen suggests that "Fitjungs" is a possessive form of "Fitjungar," which might have been a colloquial phrase that referred to the people from Fitjar (i.e. 'Fitjar' + 'ungar' = '<those> descended from Fitjar'), and that many of them may have been displaced in the aftermath of the invasion. As Fitjar was known to be a fairly affluent farming community, and the battle which displaced its inhabitants was noteworthy enough to be mentioned in a King's saga, it stands to reason that the author of this stanza would expect his contemporary listeners to be familiar with those events.

78.3: The phrase 'vánar völr' is used to mean 'a beggar's staff,' though it translates as 'staff - <of> hope (or expectation),' perhaps in the sense of an expectation for alms.

78.5: A translation of the compound 'auga-bragð' is '<of> [the] eye + sudden shift.' In some contexts, it's used to mean something happening very quickly or suddenly, i.e. in the blink of an eye, while in other contexts (particularly when paired with the prep. 'at') it's used to mean someone being 'stared' or 'glared at' (due to their doing something foolish or garnering mockery).

STANZA 79

1.) The unwise fellow,
2.) if he finally wins
3.) good wealth or woman's desire,
4.) his ambition grows,
5.) but good sense, surely not;
6.) out he goes, nose raised higher.

ORIGINAL LANGUAGE

1.) Ósnotr m[aðr]
(un+wise - person)

2.) ef eignas[k] getr
(if - <to> gain + for himself - is able)

3.) fé eð[a] fljóðs munuð.
(*wealth - or - [a] woman's - *desire)

4.) mctnaðr h[án]u[m] þ[r]óas[k]
(hubris - <in> him - grows)

5.) en man[n]vit aldregi
(but - good sense - never)

6.) f[ra]m ge[n]gr h[ann] drjúgt í dul.
(forward - goes - he - greatly - in - *aloofness)

NOTES

79.3: The noun 'fé' can mean anything from 'livestock' (generally sheep or cattle) to the more general concepts of 'property' and 'wealth.'

79.3: The noun 'munuð' can mean 'thoughts of passion or delight,' 'pleasure (in a general sense),' or more specifically 'lust.'

79.6: The noun 'dul' properly means 'concealment,' but used metaphorically, it can mean 'haughtiness, aloofness,' perhaps from a person seeming haughty and aloof when they conceal their thoughts and emotions.

STANZA 80

1.) It is amply shown,
2.) should you ask him of runes -
3.) those read by the wise, and taught,
4.) wrought by great powers,
5.) and painted by Odin -
6.) that 'tis best if he speaks naught.

ORIGINAL LANGUAGE

1.) Þ[at] e[r] þá reynt
(it - is - then - proven)

2.) e[r] þú að rúnu[m] sp[yr]r
(when - you - of - *runes - ask [him])

3.) inu[m] reginkun[n]u[m]
(the - *world+renowned)

4.) þei[m] er gerðu gin[n]regin.
(those - which - [were] made [by] - *primordial+powers)

5.) ok fáði fimbulþulr
(and - [were] drawn [by] - *great+sage)

6.) þá hef[ir] h[ann] bazt ef h[ann] þegir.
(thereupon - does - he - best - if - he - says nothing)

NOTES

80.2: The meaning here is somewhat obscure, and is translated differently by other authors. But I believe that 'you' are asking an implied individual (likely the same from the previous stanza) about 'the runes,' rather than (as some interpret) asking a question of 'the runes' themselves. This is borne out, I think, by the grammar on display, in which the runes are the indirect object, and thus leave room for an implied individual to be the missing direct object.

The noun 'rún' can have a range of meanings, including 'a mystery, secret,' 'hidden knowledge,' or even 'a proverb.' But it's most commonly used for the carved and then (sometimes) painted symbols known as runes, which formed both a system of writing and served as magical and divinatory tools. Among the ancient Norse, having knowledge of runes meant being educated and literate, attributes which may be common to the modern reader but were rare in those days.

80.3: The compound 'regin-kunnum' can mean 'world+renowned,' or perhaps '[by] the gods+known.' See further notes on 'regin' below.

80.4: The prefix of the compound 'ginn-regin' can mean 'great' or perhaps 'primordial,' while 'regin' itself can mean 'gods,' 'natural forces of the world' or even the 'world' itself. Being a pantheistic culture, the ancient Norse tended to intermix these concepts.

80.4: The manuscript appears to have a full stop (i.e. period) at the end of line 4, which is perhaps a mistake.

80.5: The term 'fimbul-þulr,' literally 'mighty/great + reciter of proverbs/sage' may be a reference to the god Odin, since he was attributed as the first to discover the runes during his act of self-sacrifice on the World Tree.

REFERENCES

In the course of translating portions of Hávamál into English, I have used the following sources of information extensively, and owe a debt of gratitude to their availability and scholarship.

Scans of the Original Manuscript
- Eddukvæði — Sæmundar-Edda; Iceland, 1260-1280 - GKS 2365 4to, [https://handrit.is].

Transcriptions of the Poetic Edda in Icelandic
- Viking Society for Northern Research, Text Series: Volume VII: Hávamál, edited by David A. H. Evans, [http://www.vsnrweb-publications.org.uk].
- Eddukvæði, Sæmundar-Edda, prepared for printing by Guðni Jónsson, [http://www.heimskringla.no].
- Edda, Die Lieder des Codex Regius nebst verwandten Denkmälern, hrsg. v. Gustav Neckel, I. Text, 5., umgearbeitete Auflage von Hans Kuhn, Heidelberg: Carl Winter 1983, [http://titus.uni-frankfurt.de].

Icelandic Dictionaries
- An Icelandic-English Dictionary, by Richard Cleasby and Gudbrand Vigfusson, [http://www.germanic-lexicon-project.org].
- A Concise Dictionary of Old Icelandic, by Geir T. Zoëga, [https://norse.ulver.com/dct/zoega].

Other Works & Authors Mentioned
- The Elder Eddas of Saemund Sigfusson, by Benjamin Thorpe.
- The Poetic Edda: The Mythological Poems, by Henry Adams Bellows.

ABOUT THE AUTHOR

Max Ingram is an author from the arid climes of Arizona. He's always loved the strange and fantastic, and has filled his life with the media and art that evoke them. He also has life-long passions for poetry, language, and Norse culture. Traveler's Rede is his third collection of poems.

www.ingramcontent.com/pod-product-compliance
Lightning Source LLC
Chambersburg PA
CBHW060752050426
42449CB00008B/1382